Also by Merlyn Vandervort

RS Means - *Repair & Remodeling Estimating Methods*, third edition – Contributing Author – Disaster Restoration Contracting

"The Ten & Ten Myth," in *The Blue Book*, 1997 international edition.

The Vandervort Report - Lake of the Ozarks Business Journal – multiple columns

Toad Life Magazine – multiple articles

Contact Merlyn Vandervort;

Merlyn@MetroRenovators.com
Merlyn@Atlasbizcoach.com

Merlyn Vandervort - Websites;

www.MerlynVandervort.com
www.MetroRenovators.com
www.Atlasbizcoach.com

Introduction

What are you going to do with your one and only life? *Make It Happen* is a step-by-step road map to help you answer that question. It provides the in-depth information, and "action steps" necessary for building a successful life and a successful business. It addresses many things that impact one's ability to reach maximum success in life; that you may not otherwise take into consideration. It also identifies the pitfalls and roadblocks that can derail one's plight for a rewarding and successful life and career.

This is a book that I've started and stopped a dozen times over the past ten years, but I'm glad I waited until now to complete it, as those ten years have been very eventful indeed. I've been very fortunate in my life, and have a lot to be thankful for. My vast experience in various businesses has afforded me many successes and challenges along the way. The Great Recession tried to suck the life right out of me, but my business and life experiences allowed me to face the eye of the hurricane head on and survive. The Great Recession cost me tens of millions of dollars, but even with such an incredible loss, I managed to survive! That which doesn't kill us makes us stronger; and I am stronger because of the challenges I've faced and overcome.

There are a number of short stories included throughout this book about successful business entrepreneurs and their life experiences, successes, failures, and challenges. History teaches us a lot if we pay attention; this book includes various events and tragedies that have shaped our history and impacted people's lives throughout the last Century. I have also included several of my life experiences, as well as successes and challenges that I think are relevant to each chapter. One can learn a lot of valuable lessons from the successes and failures of others, and this book certainly provides a lot of those valuable lessons.

If you take away only one really good thought or idea from this book, that improves your life or your business; it will surely be worth the read. If this book inspires you to set your life on course for the destiny of your choosing; it may well be the most important book you've ever read.

About the Author

Merlyn Vandervort has been a successful business entrepreneur for over twenty-five years. He is an accomplished author, motivational speaker, business consultant, and certified professional business coach. Merlyn spent the first fifteen years of his business life as a contractor rebuilding communities all over the United States, after natural disasters such as hurricanes, tornados, fires, floods, and earthquakes. His Kansas City–based construction and renovation company Metro Renovators, Inc was acquired by Inrecon/Belfor in 1998.

After fulfilling a four-year contract commitment as a regional vice president for Belfor USA, Merlyn relocated to Missouri's Lake of the Ozarks region and continued his construction and development endeavors; rebranding his construction company as Metro Renovators and Construction Services, Inc and focusing on designing and building luxury homes and high-quality commercial projects. He also focused his business attention to owning several restaurants in the Lake of the Ozarks region and in Kansas City. His hospitality successes led him to develop a $60 million, five-star resort hotel and yacht club, Camden on the Lake, adjacent to the world famous Horny Toad entertainment complex that he had developed several years earlier. Merlyn also excelled as an event promoter for such events as the National Championship Powerboat Races, the Lake of the Ozarks Bike-fest, and over a hundred benefit concerts featuring legendary recording artists such as

Willie Nelson and the Beach Boys, to name a few. The luxury resort development Vandervort founded was completed in the third quarter of 2008 amid the worst economic collapse since the Great Depression, which created a tremendous challenge; fortunately Merlyn's extensive business experience and tenacity enabled him to meet this challenge head on and overcome it.

Merlyn is still actively involved in construction and development, as well as various real estate ventures, but he now spends much of his time paying it forward by consulting and coaching other successful business owners and entrepreneurs to assist them in growing and maximizing the success of their businesses.

Contents

CHAPTER ONE

Make It Happen

What are you going to do with your one and only life?
That is a pretty serious question, and if you haven't already asked yourself that question, and answered it; maybe it's high time that you do. If this book does nothing more than get you really thinking about that question, and brings you even a little closer to answering it; it's surely worth the read.

What is it that makes the top 1 percent of the population more successful than the other 99 percent? The one simple answer is, it's the ability to make things happen! No doubt there are a lot of other factors that can enhance one's ability to reach success: money, higher education, family upbringing, and sometimes just plain luck; however the overwhelming, single most important factor in reaching that 1 percent level of success, is the ability to make things happen!

Speaking of just plain luck, there is nothing wrong with being lucky; I've met a lot of good people who are dead broke, but I have yet to meet someone I would call lucky who isn't doing well. That said, luck seldom happens by accident; luck is nothing more than the point at which preparation meets opportunity. Which means that you can *make luck happen*. If you want to be lucky, always be prepared; recognize opportunities when they present themselves to you and take advantage of those opportunities.

I find the harder I work, the more luck I seem to have.
—*Thomas Jefferson*

Consider your life a ship on a journey to your ultimate destiny. You are the captain of your ship, the master of your destiny. As that captain, you are 100 percent in control of your journey. You are responsible for the outcome of your life, responsible for the rewards as well as the hardships. If you succeed in life, it will be because you and only you *made it happen*. If you fail, it will be because you failed to make it happen. Many people will be there to assist you along the way, and many people will be there to knock you down. It is up to you to stay the course and reach the destination of your choosing. Make it happen!

What is the "it" in *Make It Happen*? The "*it*" is everything! Make everything in life happen: life, love, luck, family, health, wealth, and happiness. Whatever you want out of life, it's up to you to make it happen! Nothing happens by itself; it takes a distinct idea, followed by a plan, followed by an action, followed by another, followed by another, and so forth. It takes someone to conceive an idea, develop a plan, set action in motion, and meticulously follow up on it, working it day in and day out through to its successful conclusion. Instead of thinking of all the reasons or excuses as to why you can't do something, focus on at least one reason why you can, then implement that idea!

We live in the greatest country in the world, almost anyone in America can earn a decent living and get ahead in life if they apply themselves, take personal responsibility, and are committed to be self-reliant. In-fact there are only 5 prerequisites necessary to get ahead in life; #1 literacy, #2 hard work, #3 sobriety, #4 honesty, #5 dependability. It's a pretty simple formula; if your character possesses all five of these qualities; you will undoubtedly be able to find and hold a decent job, support yourself and your family, and be able to advance and improve the quality of your life. If you are lacking in any one of those qualities, you had better do some serious soul searching and make every effort to figure out why, because you are likely in for some rough times ahead. The harder you work, the more skills and education you obtain, and the more that people can rely on you to make things happen and get things done; is the key to creating even greater opportunity, and increases your likelihood of real success, ten-fold.

I first began my entrepreneurial endeavors swinging a hammer as a carpenter, and at the age of twenty four I started my own construction company in the back of my garage with nothing more than a pickup truck and a box of tools. I often recall how, a few years after I opened my new business, we were moving along pretty well for a small company, when all of the sudden—*bam*, in an instant, and almost overnight—I found myself on the verge of incredible opportunity to build my company into a huge success if I managed the growth correctly. In 1993, the Midwest found itself in the middle of hundred-year flood, and my company specialized in disaster cleanup and reconstruction. A catastrophic natural disaster such as a flood can be devastating to anyone who is affected by it. I've heard people say that my business profited from the misfortunes of others; while that may be true, the fact is we helped people rebuild their lives and their communities under very difficult circumstances. I quickly recognized the potential opportunity that such disasters could offer my growing company.

One of my best clients at the time of the great flood of 1993 was a third-party administrator who provided risk management services and handled losses for most of the Missouri rural schools, many of which had been severely damaged by the flood. The day of the flood, I received a phone call to go and assess the damages to several of the damaged schools. As soon as the waters receded, my company was on site, performing drying out and other emergency services. I quickly recognized that repairing the massive damage to one of the first schools I inspected would be far greater than any job I had ever completed before. I didn't have a clue how I would go about getting this magnitude of a project completed and still keep up on my other projects, let alone how I would finance this project. Contrary to what most might think, insurance companies are notoriously slow payers, and it is usually very difficult to get any progress draws. I didn't let any of that hold me back, and charged full speed ahead, figuring that things would somehow work out.

I'll never forget the day I met with the three insurance adjusters that were handling the loss. We all met out at the school and walked through the damaged site; all the while the adjusters were carefully reviewing my scope of the work, the estimate for the repairs. The loss was well over half a million dollars' worth of damage. At the end of our walk-through, the adjusters acknowledged that everything in my scope looked in order and authorized me to get started. As excited as I was, I was also scared to death, not knowing how on earth I would finance the project.

As the adjusters were getting in their car to drive back to the airport, I stopped them and said, "by the way, usually when we get into a job of this size"—yea, right, I had never done a job of that size, but I sure didn't want to tell them that—"we like to get a couple of progress draws," One adjuster asked what I thought I would need, and I replied, "I'd like to get a $100,000 draw to start with, then three or four more draws as the project progresses." He replied, "Sounds good, I'll get you a check out tomorrow." At that moment, my business and future changed forever.

That was the first of many, many large projects to come, and for the next decade there wasn't a natural disaster in North America that I wasn't at. Some people might call that lucky; I would argue that this was the moment in my life at which preparation met opportunity. I had spent several years prior to that day, preparing for that opportunity, and when it knocked on my door I recognized it, I was prepared for it, and I seized it. I made it happen!

Nothing happens by accident; sometimes the conception of an idea begins through an accidental event; the first guy who put chocolate in peanut butter may have done it by accident; but it took someone who said, "Wow, that's a great idea," then took the ball and ran with it, to invent the peanut butter cup. It didn't happen by accident; someone made it happen! He started with an idea, then formulated an action plan, developed a product, packaged it, marketed it, and now sells over a million candies every day.

Harry Burnett "H. B." Reese was a guy who knew how to make it happen; as the father of sixteen children, Reese was struggling to support his family, and in 1917 he took a job on a dairy farm owned by Milton S. Hershey, owner of the Hershey Company. Several years later Reese began working in the company's chocolate factory. He didn't know it at the time, but taking that job was the opportunity that would change his and his family's fate forever. Inspired by Hershey, and in an effort to try earning a little extra money for his family, Reese started creating his own candies in his basement, naming the candies and bars after his many children. The rest of the story is one of genuine success: Reese went on to found the H. B. Reese Candy Company and in 1963, several years after his death, his children sold the Reese Candy Company to the Hershey Company for $23.5 million, plus 5 percent of the Hershey Company; that 5 percent is now worth $1 billion. Today, nearly a hundred years later, the Reese's peanut butter cup remains one of the best-selling candies in the world.

Individuals who possess the ability to make things happen are *doers*; they do and achieve what most people might only daydream about. They get up every day with an objective to accomplish something that day and do it; they make it happen. People who make it happen don't procrastinate, don't put off until tomorrow what they can and should do today, don't dwell over the hardships life has dealt them; they adapt and overcome.

If you don't like the course your ship is headed on, only you can change it. Gleicher's Formula for change is D x V x F > R (*dissatisfaction* with how things are now, times *vision* of what is possible, times *first* real steps that can be taken toward that vision must all be greater than *resistance*). In other words, in order to effectuate real change in your life, your dissatisfaction with how your life is, combined with a vision of what your life could be and the willingness to take the first steps necessary for change, must all be greater than your resistance toward change.

Action is everything; nothing worthwhile is ever accomplished without putting action in motion. What is the action plan for your life? What's your game plan? What are you doing about it? I'm not talking about making a to-do list, I'm talking about making an action plan and putting that plan into motion.

Step 1 is knowing precisely what it is that you want out of life, and why you want it. You can't get what you want out of life if you don't first know what it is that you want. Think hard, and think big: this is your life; what do you want it to be, and why do you want it? Do you want it badly enough to be committed to it, and do you want it more than all of the resistance that has thus far kept you from pursuing it or achieving it?

Once you have figured out what it is that you want out of life, step 2 is to learn how you can achieve what it is that you want. That, however, is going to take some serious action on your part, and a commitment. Keep in mind that there is *always* action that can be taken to achieve a desired outcome. The only question is, are you determined enough to learn how to achieve your goals and then put that knowledge into an action plan and see it through? There are numerous ways to learn how to achieve what you want: school, books, seminars, mentors, work, and life experience. Be a lifelong learner!

There are four phases to learning; phase 1 is referred to as *unconscious incompetence*, which means that you are unaware of your incompetence. Phase 2 is referred to as *conscious incompetence*, which means that you are at least aware and acknowledge your lack of knowledge. Phase 3 is *conscious competence*, which means that you know something but are aware that you know it. Phase 4 is the level that you ultimately want to achieve, and that is *unconscious competence*, which means that you know something so well that it is second nature to you. Step out of your comfort zone and be a lifelong learner.

Once you know what you want out of life and have learned how to achieve it, step 3 is to make the first move toward realizing your vision; take focused and specific action to achieve what you want. This action plan must include a specific measurement of effective results; in other words, make sure that your action plan is producing effective results, and if not you need to regroup and rethink your action plan. Steps 4 through 10 are do it all again and again and again until you achieve your objective.

I emphasize training and education a lot throughout this book, and I do so for good reason because obtaining good skills and education in this world, empowers one's self to take control of their life and their destiny. I also talk a lot about higher education, because it is one of the biggest regrets of my life that I did not finish my college education or get a college degree. In full disclosure, I only spent a couple of years in college and I wasn't the best student when I was there. I had other things on my mind that I thought at the time were more important, and convinced myself that earning a college degree wasn't really for me. I couldn't have been more wrong, and in the back of my head I always knew how wrong I was. A good education and a college degree is damned important, and even much more important today than what it was thirty years ago. In-fact, call me hypocritical but I would be extremely reluctant to hire any manager to work for any one of my businesses, who doesn't have a college degree. Fortunately for me, I was able to overcome this shortcoming, but not without first graduating from the school of hard knocks, and not without taking advantage of dozens of other educational opportunities, and seminars, and surrounding myself with some really smart people. I have committed myself to being a lifelong learner, and will be until the day I pass from this earth.

What are your goals? What are you doing to achieve those goals? Are your goals SMART goals? Goals should always be *specific* (rather than I'm going to lose weight, I'm going to lose twenty pounds). Goals should always be *measurable* (I'm going to lose two pounds per week). Goals should always be *achievable* (I must be realistic; I can't lose twenty pounds in one week). Goals should always be *results oriented* (I'm going to lose twenty pounds, resulting in improved health). Goals should always be *time oriented* (I'm going to lose twenty pounds in ten weeks). Specific, measureable, achievable, results oriented, and time oriented: SMART. Write it down!

The Ford Foundation did a study finding that 23 percent of people have no idea what they want; 67 percent of people have a general idea of what they want but have no plans for how to get it; 10 percent have specific well-defined goals, but only seven out of ten of those people ever reach their goals 50 percent of the time. The top 3 percent of the people in the study reached their goals 89 percent of the time. The only difference between the top performers and the rest, was that the top 3 percent *wrote down their goals*!

Goals are directly related to the belief you have in yourself. You must first believe you can attain your goals; if you believe you can, then there is no question that—given the right effort and action plan—you can. If you believe you can't, then it is most likely that you can't. Most people fail to ever realize or live their dreams because of self-limiting beliefs. They self-sabotage their dreams because of their fear to believe.

People get into a comfort zone and have a great fear of stepping outside it. In order to step outside that comfort zone, you have to step into a learning zone, and most adults have a fear of learning what they don't already know. For example, if you grew up at any time before the technology boom of the 1990s, you may likely have a fear of learning new technology. You have to learn to step outside that comfort zone, and embrace the learning zone. Once you've embraced the learning zone, the next step is to step outside that zone into the uncomfortable zone. The uncomfortable zone is that area in your life where you are implementing your new knowledge in a whole new arena. The key is to keep yourself somewhere in between the learning zone and the uncomfortable zone— and to avoid the panic zone, which lies just outside the uncomfortable zone. Once we step into that panic zone, we tend to jump right back into our comfort zone. You can't expect positive change in your life if you aren't willing to step outside your comfort zone.

Make no excuses; you can achieve whatever it is that you want out of life, but it is up to you and only you to make it happen. Everyone's life has a story, and regardless of whatever hardship your life's history has endured, you are the only one who can change it. Make it happen!

Sarah Breedlove McWilliams Walker, better known as Madam C. J. Walker, was no stranger to the hardships of life as a young African American woman in the late 1800s. Her parents were sharecroppers who were both born into slavery and left her an orphan at the age of six. Sarah married at the age of fourteen to escape the abuses of her elder sister's husband. According to speculation, Sarah's husband was lynched or killed in a race riot, leaving Sarah a widower and single mother of a two-year-old at the age of twenty. Sarah moved from Mississippi to St. Louis, where she found work as a washerwoman. Sara never attended any school and was virtually illiterate; but she was determined to provide her daughter a better life, and put her daughter through school and even college.

Working with harsh chemicals over hot tubs as a washerwoman Sarah began to lose her hair, which caused her to experiment with finding a treatment. Inspired by a dream, Sara invented a secret formula for hair growth called "the wonderful hair grower." She then developed several other products, including a process of straightening the hair of black women that would later become known as the Walker System. Sarah and her daughter moved to Denver, where she met and married Charles J. Walker, a publicist with newspaper experience. Sarah, now using the name Madame C. J. Walker, began selling her products door to door and trained others to sell her products. In 1908 Sarah established the Lelia College in Pittsburgh to train beauticians in use of the Walker System. She later moved her company to Indianapolis, where she built a manufacturing plant and headquarters. Sarah died of a heart attack in 1919 after speaking at an anti-lynching meeting. Madam C. J. Walker became the first millionaire African American woman in America against the worst odds. She succeeded so not because she started with any advantage in life whatsoever and not because her family or the government helped her out, but because she had it within herself to make it happen!

Make it happen are words to live by in every aspect of your life—not just in your business or professional life but also in your personal life. Think hard: what is it that you really want out of life? Answer that question, then be honest and ask yourself if you are really willing to do the hard work, and put forth the effort it will take to make it happen. If you are willing to put forth the effort, then make a realistic action plan and set your life on that course; stay the course until you do make it happen!

Where are you going to be in five, ten, or twenty years? Time passes, it's going to come and go regardless; you can't control time, and you can't change the fact that it passes. What you can change, and what you can control, is what you do with your life and your time. Five years will be here in five years regardless. What is certain is that you will be five years older; what's not certain is whether you will still be in the same place in your life as you are today. You have the ability to change your life's course, but you and only you can make it happen. Time is simply a measurement of the progression of events; it's up to you to determine what that progression will be, and whether or not it is going to get you where you want to be in life and what you want to get out of life.

If there is something that you aren't happy with your life about today, what are you doing to ensure that it will be different five years from now? If you are at a dead end in your career because of a lack of education you could, with some hard work and effort, have earned a bachelor's degree in five years. Oh, wait a minute, there's the excuse as to why you can't do it: you have children to raise, you can't afford the tuition, or you're already working two jobs to make ends meet, and so on and so on. Look, it is up to you to make it happen, and if you are going to make excuses you will never make it happen. Life is tough—figure it out. There are a multitude of various grants and student loans available, joining the military and taking advantage of college resources they provide may be an option. If you have to start out with online courses that is an option. So it takes you longer than five years; maybe because of unavoidable circumstances it takes you ten years. Do you think you will be better off in your life and your career ten years from today with a college degree or without one? Those ten years are going to pass one way or the other, regardless of what you do with your time. If you want to change your life, then it's up to you and only you to make it happen!

If what you want out of life is great financial success, what have you done or what are you doing to accomplish that objective? Do you have a viable action plan, and if not, why not? Do you have the skills, training, or education to meet that objective? If not, what are you doing to obtain those skills? Do you have a great idea for a business, and if so do you have experience in that type of business? If not, what are you doing to obtain that experience? Do you have good credit? If not, what are you doing to improve it? Have you managed to save enough money to start your own business? If not, have you taken on a second or third job to enable you to do so?

If what you want out of life is love, what are you doing to make that happen? Are you the best person you can be? Do you take care of yourself? Do you make yourself happy? Are you the kind of person you would want to be with? Are you a good person? Are you honest? Are you loyal? Are you dependable? Do you have a good sense of humor? Do you have a lot to offer another person? Are you self-sufficient? These are all good qualities that everyone should look for in another person, and in turn someone should be able to expect out of you. If you fall short in any of those qualities, you need to do some serious soul searching and figure out what you need to do, and what you are able to do, to improve yourself in order to be the best person you can be, and to make yourself worthy of the kind of person you want love from.

No one can make your life happen, or cause it to turn out the way you want for it to turn out, but you! You are 100 percent responsible for the course your ship is on, and the destination you intend to arrive at. If you don't like the course you are on, it is up to you to change it; you are the captain of your ship. If life dealt you a bad hand, get over it, put it behind you, and get your ship on course. Don't waste any time crying over the battles your ship is having at sea; overcome those battles, and stay the course!

Never use being dealt a bad hand as an excuse for your position in life. Everyone has a story: bad parents, bullying, abuse, ethnicity, discrimination, poverty, lack of education, a disability, and so on and so forth. I would venture to say, that if you took a hundred people and each of them could throw their problems in the middle of the room and trade them for someone else's problems, they would each quickly want to trade back for your own problems. Deal with the life you were dealt, and don't waste any time or effort dwelling on the past or focusing on what you can't change.

You can spend your life feeling sorry for yourself, blaming your parents, your teachers, your spouse, your co-workers, your employer, or society for where you are in life; or you can get off your ass, cowboy up, and make it happen! Make your life the life you want it to be. If you are waiting around for someone else to make it happen, or to win the lottery, here's a wakeup call: your ship is headed nowhere, the pirates have taken over, and your ship is sinking fast!

Many people live their entire lives and never understand what it takes to make it happen; they either do not have the ability or they haven't put forth the effort to cultivate and develop the ability within themselves. It's too easy to blame everyone else for their plight in life, to criticize others as having had everything handed to them, or whatever other excuses makes them feel better about their own shortcomings and inabilities.

The world meets no one halfway, and the world couldn't care less about what you make of your life. It's all on you, and once you accept and understand that, you are ready to begin your journey. If you're afraid of change, turn that fear into faith; faith leads to action, and action leads to change! If it were easy, anyone could do it, but if it were easy, it wouldn't be worthwhile, and it certainly wouldn't pay very well.

America is full of people's success stories, and the one common denominator in all of those success stories, the one thing that those people all have or had in common, isn't wealth, education, or heritage; it is that they all had the ability to overcome tremendous odds and adversity, to reach down into their hearts and souls, and make it happen!

One of my favorite success stories is that of Alex Manoogian. A Turkish immigrant who fled Turkey to escape a life of persecution, in 1920, at the age of 19, Manoogian arrived at Ellis Island with only fifty dollars, two suitcases, and the resolve to someday bring his family to the United States. The one advantage he had, other than his unrelenting drive to excel, was that his family had instilled in him at an early age a great emphasis on education and enterprise. Manoogian settled in Detroit and purchased a couple of used machines that he repaired; he then started producing machined parts for the Detroit auto industry; this was the beginning of Masco. Wearing every hat in the company, from press operator, estimator, and foreman to CEO, Manoogian began a real American success story.

In the early 1950s an inventor brought Manoogian a single-handled water faucet that featured a ball valve that allowed the combination of volume with mixed hot and cold water. Although the faucet leaked, it was easy to operate and Manoogian recognized the potential, the opportunity; he purchased the inventor's rights to the faucet. He improved the design, and in 1954 he patented and produced the first successful washer less ball valve faucet—the Delta faucet, named for its faucet cam shape, similar to the fourth letter of the Greek alphabet. The overwhelming response to this incredible innovation generated the revenues needed for Masco to expand its operations, and ultimately become the largest building supply manufacturer in the United States.

Alex Manoogian definitely had what it takes to make it happen. His life story eventually had an important impact on my life's story. In the mid-1990s Masco acquired a considerable position in Inrecon LLC, which at the time was the largest restoration company in the United States. And in 1998 Inrecon acquired my construction company, Metro Renovators. Soon later Masco acquired 100 percent of the company, and later sold it to Belfor USA, which is now the largest restoration company in the world.

The stories of H. B. Reese, Sarah Walker, and Alex Manoogian are just a few of the thousands of American success stories. Young Americans, who against great adversity, against all odds, and with nothing but their own hearts and souls and their own blood, sweat, and tears, created something out of nothing. Nothing was given to them; their parents didn't do it for them; the government didn't subsidize them, their families, or their businesses; they and they alone made it happen! Reese was jobless, with sixteen mouths to feed; Walker was an illiterate orphan; and Manoogian arrived in America with nothing more than a few dollars and a suitcase; all of these exceptional entrepreneurs turned adversity into fortune beyond most people's imaginations. The one common denominator they all possessed wasn't wealth or education; it was the ability to make it happen!

Are you a make it happen person? It's not a hard question; you either are or you aren't. If you aren't, do you want to be? Do you have what it takes inside of you, and are you willing to put forth whatever effort it takes?

The world meets no one halfway; it's up to you to make it happen! Nothing ventured, nothing gained.

)Action Steps

1. Define what it is that you want out of your personal life and why you want it. Knowing what you want out of life is the first step toward achieving it.

2. Define what it is that you want out of your professional life, career, or business.

3. List three things that you can do in the near future to put yourself on the path toward realizing what you want out of your personal life.

4. List three things that you can do in the near future to put you on the path to realizing what you want out of your professional life, career, or business.

Before we can reach for our dreams, we must first identify them and identify what action we can take to reach them. Believe in your dream; commit yourself from this day forward to learning whatever you need to learn to make that dream a reality and do it. Take quantified action every day, day after day; to implement what you have learned, stay focused like a laser and realize your dreams. Make it happen!

Write down your responses to these action steps before you move on to the next chapter.

CHAPTER TWO

Protect Yourself

Protect yourself—what does that mean? Protect yourself in all aspects of life. Protect yourself, and protect your family. Protect your estate, your assets, your reputation, your person, your health and well-being. If you are in business, protect your business, protect your image, protect your customers, and protect your employees. If you don't protect yourself, no one else will!

Now that you have decided that you are going to *make it happen* and be a success at life and in business, you have set your life on course for a challenging and rewarding journey. Your ship has now left the port. As the captain of your ship, you have set the course to your destiny. Now it's time to protect your ship (yourself) and your cargo (everything important to you: your family, your wealth, your business). Make no mistake: the better your ship, and the more valuable your cargo, the more likely it is that you will be attacked by pirates trying to steal the cargo, sink the ship, and prevent you from reaching your destination. As the captain, it is your responsibility to make sure that doesn't happen; no one else is going to do that for you.

First and foremost, establish a good professional team. Make sure you have a good attorney and a good accountant; you might also consider enlisting the aid of a good professional business coach. Choose each of these professionals very carefully. Choose professionals who come highly recommended, and make sure that you trust them and get along well with them. These professionals will likely be very valuable advisers for many years to come, and can be very helpful in protecting you, your family, your estate, and your business.

After you have chosen your team of professionals, get your ship in order. Make sure you have a will; determine with your attorney and accountant whether you need a trust and if so what kind of trust. Make sure you have adequate life insurance, and determine who should own the policy (you, your spouse, or a trust), who your beneficiaries are, and how you would want your estate divided in the event of your or your spouse's passing. If you have children who are minors make sure you have a plan in place in the unfortunate event that both you and your spouse pass at the same time. Understand the tax consequences of your estate or trust, and how they will affect your beneficiaries.

Make sure you have a good insurance agent, and carefully evaluate all your insurance needs and policies. Make sure your assets are adequately insured. Strongly consider an all-risk personal umbrella policy, making sure you have adequate liability coverage. Understand your homeowner's policy, and be very cautious of an actual cash value policy, as it will likely only cover the used or depreciated replacement cost of anything lost as opposed to new item or guaranteed replacement costs.

Don't be your own worst financial enemy; make a budget, put that budget on paper, and stick to it. Don't live beyond your means. Credit cards should be paid off in full every month or used only in an emergency. Prioritize what you need, then evaluate what you want. Work with your accountant to make sure you understand your tax liabilities, and evaluate what you might be able to do to lower them.

Plan for a rainy day; the rule of thumb is that you should have six months to a year's worth of your expenses in a reserve account that is off limits and can only be accessed in the case of a dire emergency. On a much smaller scale, you may also consider keeping a small cash reserve on hand in an easily accessible safe place. You never know what challenges life may throw at you, and a financial reserve is not only a must for protecting yourself but will also give you peace of mind.

Plan for the future. Whatever your age, if you have kids they will be in college before you know it, and if you ask anyone who is already retired, they will tell you that that time came in the blink of an eye. Never plan on a social safety net; if you are going to protect yourself, it's up to you and only you to provide for your future. If you have an employer-matched retirement fund, make sure to at least contribute the maximum amount that your employer is matching. Never take out a thirty-year mortgage. Use the shortest amortization (number of years to pay your mortgage) that your budget can afford; this may reduce the interest rate of your loan, and will definitely create substantial equity much faster than putting the amount of the increased payment difference into a savings account. For example, a $250,000 loan at 6 percent interest amortized over thirty years has a monthly payment of $1,498.88. The same loan amortized over fifteen years has a monthly payment of $2,109.65; the monthly payment only increases by $610.77, but the mortgage is paid off in half the time and saves you a total of $159,860!

Protect your credit rating at all costs. A poor credit rating makes you a bad risk to creditors, and greatly inhibits your ability to succeed and get ahead in life. Credit is difficult if not impossible to get without a good credit rating, and any credit you might get will only be at a high-risk interest rate, which could easily double the amount of payments you would have with good credit. Understand your credit report, and check it frequently. If there is any negative information on your credit report, make it a priority to remedy it and improve your rating.

Ours is a very tumultuous world; it is always changing, and not always for the best. Bad economic times often bring out the worst in people, and that greatly increases the odds of you or someone in your family being the victim of a crime, fraud, or other form of abuse. It's not a matter of whether you or one of your loved ones will be a victim of some crime at some point in the future; that is extremely likely; the unknown is when will it happen and how serious it will be. Will the crime be against you or your loved ones? Will it be limited to only financial damages, or could it include emotional or bodily harm? Don't give anyone the benefit of the doubt. Trust your instincts and your own intuition.

Something that most people don't know about me is that I used to compete in rodeos, and one of my specialties was bull riding. When I was much younger, I trained for two seasons with the legendary Jim Shoulders, who at the time was in *Guinness book of World Records* as the most successful rodeo cowboy in history, with sixteen world titles. I'll never forget the advice that Jim always gave us: "Boys, if you're going to be in this business, there is one thing you know for certain, and two things you don't know; the one thing you know for sure is that you are going to get hurt, the two things you don't know is when or how bad." The day after hearing that, I watched one of my teammates get his nose ripped off his face by the horn of a Brahma bull. As the poor guy was laying on his back, half conscious, with blood spewing from his face, Jim's words of wisdom to him were, "Sonny, I've had my nose broke seven times, and it hurt just as bad every time." The moral of this story is that things happen in life, and sometimes bad things happen; when they do, we must pick ourselves back up, dust ourselves off, and get back on the bull. I've always found this to be a valuable lesson that can easily be related to all aspects of life; life can be hard, and if you are going to put yourself out there at all, you are going to have to take a risk, and sooner or later you are likely going to get hurt; the real question is when and how bad?

Technology has created a plethora of new risks in life, and it seems that technology is changing every day; you can barely purchase a new computer or cell phone without it being outdated by the time you get it home. Technology has brought a lot of great things to our lives, but it has also brought a lot of bad things and created many new risks. If you are like the many people—over half the population, in fact—who grew up before the technology boom of the 1990s your technology skills may be limited. This can make you much more at risk to tech-savvy criminals.

Protect yourself and your family from Internet-based fraud and from being duped by unsavory people who prey on the naive and overly trusting. Avoid continued Internet contact with anyone you haven't actually met in person and have a good degree of trust in. Be very careful about anything you put on the Internet, including photos, because they will likely be there forever. Children are especially at risk, and should have strict safety guards in place to protect them from online predators.

In 2012 an extremely cruel online prank made the headlines. A twenty-eight-year-old New Zealand woman systematically created profiles for fictional teenage girls looking for love and flirting with unsuspecting young men. People making up fake profiles and scamming others into fake relationships has become pretty commonplace on the Internet, but here is the cruel twist to this particular prank: she would have each of the phony girls coerce these naive young men into a romantic online relationship, and then kill off each of the fake girls in a terrible accident just to reveal the mourning that the distraught young men exhibited online as a result of the tragedy. The *Sydney Morning Herald* reported that an estimated forty young men were victims of this cruel prank. Every day, kids are at the risk of adults wishing to do them harm for their own sick and perverted reasons. Online bullying resulting in teen suicide is unfortunately happening more and more every year. Protect yourself and protect your family. This is just one example of how easily people can be harmed by unscrupulous people praying on them via the internet.

Identity fraud costs consumers billions of dollars every year, but the financial devastation victims incur is often the least of their problems, and they can easily find themselves spending months if not years trying to undo the damage that has been done to them. Some people never recover from the damages caused by identity fraud.

Take the case of Britney Ossenfort of Orange County, Florida, who had met and befriended a woman named Michelle through mutual friends, and the two soon became roommates. At first Brittney tried to overlook some of Michelle's seemingly odd behavior, but alarm bells started sounding the more Michelle tried to look like and simulate Britney by dressing like her, dying her hair and changing its style to match Britney's, and even getting a matching tattoo. It all came to a head the day Britney received a call at work to come and bail herself out of jail; it seems that Britney had been charged with prostitution. But Britney wasn't Britney at all; Michelle had used Britney's identity, had given Britney's name and stolen identification to the police. To add insult to injury, investigators soon discovered that Michelle wasn't really even Michelle at all. In fact, Michelle's real name was Richard Phillips. Richard was a transgender man who had been living as a woman long before Britney or their mutual friends had ever met Michelle. To make matters even worse for the real Brittney, even after the police had cleared up the identity fraud, her name could not be removed from the arrest record. Apparently, once an inmate is booked into jail in Orange County, whatever name that person is booked under cannot be changed.

Have you ever had your purse or wallet stolen, or your vehicle broken into? Well, that is where Anndorie Sachs's nightmare began. Anndorie was the mother of four and enrolled at the University of Utah when she received a call from child protective services informing her that she was under investigation because her newborn baby tested positive for methamphetamines. Sachs was quite concerned and confused because she hadn't given birth to a child in over a year and had never used methamphetamines. Child protective services refused to believe her story and opened an in-depth investigation into her life that involved her employer, her family, and even in the interrogation of her four children.

This so-called investigation did not initially involve a medical exam or a DNA test which could have easily cleared up the matter. Finally the investigation revealed that Sachs had recently had her vehicle broken into and her driver's license had been stolen by a pregnant meth addict who took the stolen license and gave it to the hospital where she gave birth to her drug-addicted child, even using the false name on the child's birth certificate. Child protective services was very slow to believing Sachs's story, and finally did do a DNA test to prove once and for all that the child didn't belong to Sachs. Unfortunately that still didn't stop the hospital from pursuing collection efforts from Sachs. This nightmare may never be over for Anndorie Sachs and her family; identity fraud can continue to cause havoc in one's life for many years to come. What about the infant baby who was born addicted to drugs? The baby may have never known who her real mother and father were, as their names weren't even indicated on the birth certificate, leaving her as a drug-addicted infant to be placed in the foster care system.

Millions of frivolous lawsuits are filed every year. All it takes is someone wanting what you have. The more you have to get, the more likely it is that you are going to have people coming after what you have. They don't need a reason, just an excuse. Most people don't realize that anyone can file a lawsuit against anyone for just about anything. Rather you can win the lawsuit or not is often irrelevant; the costs in defending yourself, and the damage to your reputation—not to mention the personal and emotional drain that litigation can have on a person or a business—can be overwhelming. Regardless of how frivolous the suit might be, it has to be defended; if it is not, the person filing the suit against you will likely be awarded a settlement, and a judgment will be imposed on you or your business. A judgment can not only ruin your credit but can also allow someone to empty your bank accounts and garnish your wages.

Defending any legal action is extremely costly, and unfortunately the same exorbitant costs may not equally apply to the party who files the suit. Unscrupulous litigation attorneys will often take on any case that they think they can squeeze a dollar out of and will often accept the case on a contingency basis (being paid a certain percentage of the settlement), especially if the person being sued has substantial resources or insurance coverage. The overwhelming majority of cases are settled out of court, and often settled simply because it is cheaper to settle a case than to continue paying the extensive cost of litigation. The moral of this story is to avoid litigation at all costs because the only ones who ever really make out are the attorneys!

It's just like the lesson I learned from my rodeo coach, Jim Shoulders; if you are in business or are successful, the one thing that is certain is that at some point or another you are going to get sued; the two things you don't know is when it will happen or how bad it will hurt.

Speaking of frivolous lawsuits, you may remember this one. Washington, D.C., judge Roy Pearson Jr. sued a local dry cleaner for misplacing a pair of his trousers, arguing that he never received the same-day service or satisfaction guaranteed that was advertised by the mom-and-pop owners of Custom Cleaners. Pearson sought satisfaction the way only an overeducated lawyer could: he filed a $67 million lawsuit against store proprietors Soo and Jin Chung for an $800 pair of pants (he later lowered his demand to $54 million. The Chungs offered to settle out of court for $12,000, but Pearson refused. Fortunately the court ruled against Pearson, and his subsequent appeal was rejected. This just goes to show that any idiot can sue decent, hardworking businesspeople for just about any amount.

Perhaps the most famous frivolous lawsuit is *Liebeck v. McDonald's*, the case in which eighty-year-old Stella Liebeck spilled a McDonald's coffee in her lap, causing third-degree burns on her legs, lap, and groin area. Liebeck was quickly criticized about the suit before most knew the whole story. After all, coffee is supposed to be hot. However, McDonald's has had numerous complaints filed concerning the scalding temperatures of its coffee, which is served between 180 and 190 degrees for optimum flavor. To put that into perspective, coffee at most restaurants is served at around 140 degrees. Liebeck only sued McDonald's for the actual costs of medical expenses related to her injuries, but McDonald's refused to pay the medical bills, most likely trying to avoid setting any precedent. Ultimately, the jury awarded Liebeck $2.7 million. As a business, McDonald's should have protected itself from this type of lawsuit and should have taken corrective action over the temperature of its coffee long before, as it had already received over seven hundred complaints. The company should also have better protected itself and settled out of court, paying only the small amount of Liebeck's medical bills.

Filing a lien is similar to filing a lawsuit. In most states, anyone can file a lien against anyone else's property for just about anything he or she chooses. All it takes is filling out a simple form, and paying a minimal filing fee. As a contractor I have had experience with unscrupulous subcontractors causing liens to be filed against various properties. On more than one occasion I have paid, for example, concrete contractors for work they have done for me on a project for which I was the general contractor, only to find out six months later that they neglected to pay their concrete suppliers and falsified the lien waiver they supplied me, which indicated that they had paid their suppliers. As a result, I was forced to pay the concrete suppliers for concrete that I had already paid the subcontractors for. I've also had unscrupulous subcontractors try to overbill me (which is ultimately overbilling my client) for services beyond the scope of our contract, and for work or costs never agreed to. Sure, I could file suit against the subcontractor (and have, on occasion), and I would ultimately prevail, but in that case it would be my client in the meantime who would suffer with an unjust lien against his or her property. The only alternative is to put up a 150 percent bond in order to get the lien released. In other words, if for any reason a subcontractor says that he or she is due $10,000, regardless if it is true or not, I would have to either pay the unscrupulous subcontractor or put up a $15,000 bond until I am able to succeed in a drawn-out court battle. Here is the real kicker: subcontractors don't even have to prove that they ever did any work on said property; they only have to *say* that they did.

Accidents happen. You should always make every effort to prevent them, but there is nothing that you can do to prevent all of them. Many accidents are beyond your control, but that doesn't mean that someone isn't going to try and hold you liable for them. Make certain that you have adequate insurance coverage for all risks that you, your family, and your business may have exposure to. Never be so foolish as to think that some catastrophic incident can't happen to you. In both my personal life as well as my business I have experienced devastating losses that would have completely wiped me out if I hadn't had the proper insurance coverage. My family and I have been victims of a tragic fire to our home and lost everything we owned. On another occasion, while building a large superstructure facility, my construction business experienced a tragic loss of life in a fluke construction accident when one of our valued subcontractors accidentally fell down a stairwell shaft to his death. Unfortunately, accidents happen, and you need to be prepared and protect yourself.

In the words of Donald Trump, "I love you—sign this." Prenuptial agreements are always a very touchy topic for couples in love and contemplating matrimony. No one ever gets married with the thought of ever getting divorced. The unfortunate reality, however, is that the only things that fail almost as often as businesses do are marriages. Fifty percent of all marriages end in divorce, which means that you have at least a 50 percent chance of losing half of your wealth if you don't protect yourself. Let's face it, right, wrong, or indifferent, people change; you don't always know the person you're marrying until after you're married. If you've already experienced a divorce, have children with your first spouse, and are contemplating a second marriage, your children certainly need to be a big part of that consideration. Some people falsely see a prenup as making it too easy to get a divorce; I would suggest that it makes it much easier to stay happily married, because you have the peace of mind of knowing that the person who married you did so for love, not money, and you don't have the potential threat of losing half of your life's assets hanging over your head. Any divorce attorney will tell you that if you are a successful person without a prenup it's cheaper to get out now rather than later; half of what you have today is far less than half of what you are likely to have two or three years from now. That threat alone could be incentive enough to get a divorce rather than putting forth the time and effort to make a marriage work. A prenuptial agreement is nothing more than an agreement between two responsible adults that, in the unfortunate event things don't work out the way they both intend, this is how they will part company and divide assets, period. If you have children from a previous relationship, or own a business, it would be irresponsible as a parent or a business owner to not protect yourself, your children, and your business from the devastation that will certainly be caused by a tumultuous divorce.

Whether you work for a company, manage a company, or own a company, a good understanding of human resource management and workplace laws is imperative. Every company should have good and enforced policies regarding the workplace. Harassment and discrimination should never be tolerated in the workplace—by either the employee or employer.

Never say, write, text, e-mail, or do anything that you wouldn't want anyone in the world to see. Be very careful and thoughtful about whatever you say or write; the world is a viral place, and privacy is practically nonexistent. In today's world, everyone has a cell phone, and most cell phones have the ability to record just about anything in any format. A good rule of thumb is, if you would have difficulties explaining what you communicate; to your spouse, your family, your friends, your customers, your employer, employees, or a jury: don't say it, write it, text it, e-mail it, or do it!

Never be as foolish or arrogant as to believe that text messages, e-mails, or any other form of correspondence will be kept in confidence.

Just ask disgraced former New York congressman Anthony Weiner, who resigned from the US House of Representatives after texting inappropriate photos to women he thought he could trust to keep them in confidence. On second thought, Weiner might not be such a good person to ask; even after giving up his congressional seat he tried to run for mayor of New York City and obviously hadn't learned his lesson, because he kept up the same foolish behavior and couldn't even get more than 5 percent of the vote.

Avoid any correspondence or communications with anyone if your judgment is at all impaired by drugs or alcohol. If you've ever sent or received a late-night text, e-mail, or phone call that you wish you hadn't sent or received, you know why this a bad idea.

Pretty much any written or recorded communications are discoverable evidence in a court of law. Deleted e-mails are only deleted on your computer, and can still be retrieved from your Internet service provider. If you don't want the whole world to see it, keep it to yourself.

Read everything you sign carefully. Know what you are signing, why you are signing it, what the ramifications of your signature are, and how you should sign any document. If you have any question about the legal consequences of your signature, consult an attorney. Anything that requires your signature is a contract; you are legally committing yourself to some obligation, and if you fail to meet that obligation, there are likely to be consequences for breaching the agreement. Make damn sure you completely understand what it is you are signing, what obligation you are committing too, and what the ramifications are if you fail to follow through on your commitment.

Understand the capacity under which you are signing any documents. Are you signing it personally, or are you signing it as a representative of a company or organization? If you are signing any document in a representative capacity, make sure that your signature is followed by your title as well as what organization you are signing for (example: John Smith, manager, ABC Enterprises, Inc.). Failing to properly sign any document including the title and organization can potentially create personal liability for you if the agreement is ever breached. Also, make certain that the organization you are signing for is a legally established entity in the state in which it conducts business. Failing to do so can create an ambiguity in who is actually responsible for the agreement, which could also potentially create a personal liability for the signatory. Be very cautious about signing any personal guarantees, and never sign a personal guarantee for a business that you don't own and completely control.

If you own your own business, maintaining a separation between yourself and your business can help protect both. Get together with your attorney and your accountant to determine what legal entity would best suit your needs. Filing as a C corporation, Subchapter S corporation, or limited liability company may be the answer to help legally separate you from your business and provide some shelter for you and your family in the event your business fails or is jeopardized by litigation. You may also consider having one entity own all of the property and assets and leasing it to another entity as a management company. This may assist in further separating your business assets from the risk of litigation. Never forget that anyone, for just about any reason, can file a lawsuit against you or your business, so it is incumbent on you to protect yourself, your business, and your assets.

Protecting yourself also means defending yourself and your family. I understand the gun control debate, but regardless of which side of the issue your moral compass falls on, you should be prepared to defend yourself, your property and your family from those who would do you harm given the opportunity. One need only hear the story of eighteen-year-old mother Sarah McKinley to understand the importance of this issue. McKinley was widowed on Christmas Eve 2011, when she lost her husband to cancer. According to McKinley's account of events, Justin

Martin had been prowling around her home in the days following her husband's funeral, and on New Year's Eve he and accomplice Dustin Stewart aggressively tried to break into McKinley's home. McKinley had barricaded herself into the house and immediately called 911 from her bedroom, with her infant baby by her side. She spoke with the 911 operator for over twenty minutes, awaiting a police response, while the intruders were determined to get into her house. McKinley told the operator that she was armed with a twelve-gauge shotgun and a pistol, and wanted to know if it was OK for her to shoot the intruders if they made it into her bedroom. The operator hesitated with a reply, and McKinley asked a second time. The operator finally replied, "I can't tell you that you can do that, but you do what you have to do to protect your baby." Moments later the intruder Martin kicked the door in, and charged at her with a knife. McKinley didn't hesitate and shot and killed the intruder before he could get to her or her infant child. Martin's alleged accomplice, Dustin Stewart, fled when he heard the gunshot, and later surrendered to police. He was charged with burglary, and later charged with Martin's murder, even though he never fired a shot; since his accomplice was killed in the commission of a felony, he was complicit of murder.

I can speak on this topic with some authority; when I was growing up, my parents owned a small motel style apartment complex in a suburb of south Kansas City Missouri. After my parents divorced, my mother ingrained herself in the property management business, and I soon found myself spending much of my after school time and weekends, fixing up and maintaining these rental properties. I guess I could say that this is where I first learned construction and property renovation. You might say I had quite an interesting childhood; this early life experience also taught me a lot about business and people. In any event, at one point during the late 1970's my mother managed several apartment buildings in some depressed areas of midtown Kansas City. When I was fifteen years old, my mother was shot twice in the stomach with a 38 caliber pistol by a woman who was suspected of breaking into someone's apartment. Fortunately my mother recovered from the tragedy without any permanent disability. Two years later, when I was only seventeen years old, I was assisting my mother with an eviction when I was attacked and stabbed with a knife. While I was able to get the knife away from the assailant and subdue him, his wife proceeded to get a gun and was intent on shooting both me and my mother. Fortunately there was an off duty deputy sheriff in a neighboring apartment and he was able to take the couple into custody without further escalation of the traumatic situation. An ambulance was able to get me to the hospital before I had lost an excessive amount of blood, and I quickly recovered. No doubt these events were very serious lessons to me at a very early age in life, that there are very bad people in this world who can and will do you harm, and the importance of being prepared and able to defend and protect yourself if need be.

There are thousands of other similar stories that should give everyone pause; unfortunately the world is full of bad people who will do us or our families harm if given the opportunity, and it is incumbent upon a prudent person to be prepared to protect ourselves by whatever means necessary, or at least by whatever means one can live with. My mom was a single mother of five, just trying to do her job to support her family, and she was shot in the process. I was just a teenage kid helping my mom after school, when some crazy guy twice my age viciously attacked me and stabbed me with a knife. Sarah McKinley's attackers weren't even armed with a gun, but it didn't stop them from a home invasion, and attacking a young widowed mother and her infant child. I cringe to think what might have happened to Sarah and her child if she hadn't been prepared to protect herself. If Sarah McKinley's story doesn't send chills up your spine, I'm not sure what will.

I'm not suggesting that everyone goes out and buys a gun, because a gun in the hands of someone who isn't trained how to use it can be just as dangerous as not having any means of protection at all. I am suggesting however that you give some serious thought as to how you would defend yourself and your family if the need ever arises. Take self-defense classes, get a good security alarm system, keep a can of mace handy, a good dog is seldom ever a bad idea, and yes getting the proper training for handling and using a fire arm, or carrying a concealed weapon can be a responsible option. Put forth a lot of effort to make yourself consciously aware of your surroundings, and all situations; trust your gut instinct.

It's better to be judged by twelve of your neighbors than carried by six of your friends.

)Action Steps

1. Do a self-evaluation to determine where you may be vulnerable.

2. Locate and review all of your insurance policies.

3. If you don't already have a will, get with an attorney and make one up.

4, If you don't already have a good attorney or a good accountant, do your due diligence and cultivate these professional relationships.

5. If you are in business for yourself, and don't already have a good professional business coach, do your due diligence and locate one.

6. Examine what you can and should be doing to better protect yourself, your business, and your family.

Prepare yourself and protect yourself. Don't kid yourself; sooner or later you will face a very real and present threat against you, your family, or your business. This threat may be legal, monetary, or worse. Unfortunately, you will not know when it will happen; you will not know how bad the threat is until it happens, and if you aren't prepared at that point, it will be too late.

Make yourself a note to prioritize these action steps once you have finished this book.

CHAPTER THREE

Do It Right

Do it right; that sounds like a pretty simple instruction, but what does it really mean? Again, the "it" is everything in life. Do everything—in life, love, family, and business—right or don't do it at all. What's right is usually self-evident; if you have to ask if its right it probably isn't.

You are the captain of your ship. Start by building that ship well. If you have planned a destiny of high aspirations, it's going to be a long and challenging journey, so you'd better make sure that you have built a ship that can withstand the rough waters and reach your destination so that you can reap the rewards of your efforts. Do yourself right—be the best person you can be. Be the captain that people will follow into battle. Be the captain that people can depend on, the captain that people respect. Be strong in mind, body, and heart. Never pass up an opportunity to improve yourself, gain knowledge, or make yourself a better captain.

Live a long and healthy life; make sure that you are around long enough to enjoy the life you have built for yourself. Live long enough to raise your kids, play with your grandchildren and great-grandchildren, and reach the destination you have set for your life. When you're young, thinking about your health is probably not at the top of your priorities; you're still full of vim and vigor and thinking that life lasts forever, that you're invincible. As you start growing older, you soon realize that life doesn't last forever and that you aren't invincible. The sooner you start taking care of your health, the better. Watch your diet, be cautious of everything you put in your body; you don't want to overload your ship, because it will definitely slow you down, and could potentially sink your ship before you reach your destination. If you're not exercising, get off your butt, and start walking. If you're a smoker, stop; it's killing you long before your time. If you're doing drugs, quit; finish reading this book and get high on life! Do it right!

No matter how smart you already are, or already think you are, your brain no doubt has the capacity to absorb a hundred times the amount of knowledge that it already has. Why would you ever want to leave that much of your brain empty? Your brain is a sponge and will take on as much information as you will feed it; fill it full of knowledge every day. Your brain is also a muscle, and the more you exercise it the better it works; exercise your brain every day, and exercise it vigorously. Get educated: go to college, read books, attend seminars, stay up on current events. Education gives you knowledge, and knowledge is power—the power you'll need to fuel your ship and become the master of your destiny.

Don't just do right by your family; do your family right! You can't choose your parents, and you can't choose your siblings; those we are all stuck with. We can either be thankful that our parents did family right or get over the fact that they didn't and not make the same mistakes ourselves. Fortunately we do get to choose the person we plan to spend the rest of our lives with, and we do have a significant say with how our children are raised and how they will turn out. This is something that you had better get right. When you bring children into this world, it's your responsibility to raise them into good-hearted, educated, hardworking, and productive adults. You have a very short window of time to get parenting right, and getting it right makes your life's journey much smoother than the alternative.

One of the biggest problems with society today, is unwanted or unplanned children being brought into this world, or bringing a child into this world when the parents have no ability to care for a child, and expect someone else or society to do it for them. Take every possible precaution and make every effort to not have children until you are secure in your life, and ready to bring a child into this world. Make every effort to not have a child out of wedlock. A child very much needs both of their parents in their life, and both parents need to support one another at every turn in providing for, and raising a child. It's very difficult to be a good parent, if you're not first grown up and self-sufficient yourself.

My parenting advice would be to always be 100 percent consistent. This starts as soon as you bring your child into the world, with something as minute as an early and consistent bedtime to a firm no always meaning no. Discipline your children when necessary, but never scream or curse at your kids; and if they do need a spanking, always follow it up with a hug and reassurance of love. Always be supportive of your kids, but never allow for them to become codependent. Your children have enough friends growing up; they don't need another friend, what they need is a parent. Be a parent! You'll have plenty of time to be your children's friend after they are all grown up. The best reward in life is to raise your kids to become loving, self-sufficient, self-reliant, and productive adults.

What is it that you want out of life? If you haven't figured that out, I'd suggest you start doing some serious soul searching; think hard and figure it out. Be realistic, but be bold. Surely everyone has asked themselves at some point or another, if I had three wishes in life, what would they be? Stop reading for a second and ask yourself that question, and write down the answers. Think big!

#1_____ #2_____ #3_____

Anything worth wanting or wishing for is certainly worth writing down. Now ask yourself what you are doing about making those three wishes a reality. If those are really the top three things you want out of life, the three things that you would wish for in life if only you had the opportunity, today is your opportunity. Make those three wishes, but instead of waiting around for some genie to pop out of a bottle and hand them to you, or praying that someday you win the lottery, make an action plan today to make those wishes a reality, then get up every day with those three wishes in mind, and make them happen! By the way, my three wishes in life are for health, wealth, and happiness.

Whoever said money doesn't buy happiness never had any money; whoever said money isn't everything may have been right; money may not be everything, but it's a heck of a lot better than whatever is. Money can't buy you love, but without it love often fades away pretty quickly. I would agree that money isn't everything and there are obviously many more important things in life—namely, your family. However, if you love your family and are the one responsible for its security and well-being, money quickly becomes damned important. Who doesn't want his or her family to live in a nice neighborhood, and have nice things? Who doesn't want to send his or her children to a good school and then off to college? Who doesn't want to be able to enjoy retirement? If people don't think that all of those things are important, they're kidding themselves. All of this quality of life requires a substantial amount of money, and creating this quality of life doesn't come easily and it certainly doesn't happen by accident. If you want this quality of life, it is up to you and only you to make it happen for you and your family! Do your life right!

When my oldest son was about ten, my brother-in-law asked him what he wanted to be when he got older; my son had always previously answered that question with "A contractor, like my dad." But this time he answered the question with "When I get older I want to be king." My brother-in-law smiled and tried to explain to my son that in America we don't have a monarchy so he couldn't be king, but he could aspire to be a politician and possibly the president. My reply to my son was; "Son, if you want to be a king, you have to first build yourself a kingdom." Does anyone really believe that Warren Buffett isn't the king of Berkshire Hathaway, or Bill Gates isn't the king of Microsoft, or Oprah Winfrey isn't the Queen of Harpo Productions and talk television? These three American icons definitely did it right and built their own empires—their own kingdoms, if you will. And in doing so they have amassed fortunes equal to or greater than that of any royal monarchy.

Other than the ability to make it happen, the one other quality that the world's most successful people understand is that whatever they do they have to do it right. Did you ever see anyone get wealthy and build a successful business by doing it poorly or trying to sell a bad product? No, it doesn't work that way. Sure, there are a lot of hustlers out there making a buck or two swindling people; but those people are doomed for failure, prison, or early death. Anything worth doing is worth doing right, and if you can't do it right then you might as well not do it at all! That doesn't necessarily mean that everything you do right will automatically be a success; there are always risks, and unforeseen obstacles, and timing can be everything. But if you do something right, the likelihood of success is a hundredfold greater of success than it is with something that isn't done right. I would add that if you do something right, do it with quality and integrity; there will always be a market for it.

Harley-Davidson—the American motorcycle manufacturing company founded in 1903 in Milwaukee, Wisconsin, by William S. Harley,

Arthur Davidson, Walter Davidson, and William A. Davidson—could be called the poster child for lessons well learned in doing it right. Harley-Davidson (HD) was one of only two major American motorcycle manufacturers to survive the Great Depression.

Beginning in 1901, William S. Harley, age twenty, drew up plans for a small engine with a displacement of 7.07 cubic inches (116 cc), and 4-inch (102 mm) flywheels. The engine was designed for use in a regular pedal-bicycle frame. Over the next two years, Harley and his childhood friend Arthur Davidson worked on their "motor-bicycle" using the machine shop at the home of their friend Henry Melk on Milwaukee's North Side. It was finished in 1903 with the help of Arthur's brother Walter Davidson. Upon testing their "power-cycle," Harley and the Davidson brothers found it unable to climb the hills around Milwaukee without pedal assistance. They quickly wrote off their first motor-bicycle as a valuable learning experiment.

Not letting their first failure hold them back, they immediately began work on a new and improved second-generation machine. This first "real" Harley-Davidson motorcycle had a bigger engine of 24.7 cubic inches (405 cc) with 9.75-inch (25cm) flywheels weighing twenty-eight pounds (13 kg). The machine's advanced loop-frame pattern was similar to the 1903 Milwaukee Merkel motorcycle (designed by Joseph Merkel, later of Flying Merkel fame). The bigger engine and loop-frame design took it out of the motorized bicycle category and marked the path to future motorcycle designs. The young men also received help with their bigger engine from outboard motor pioneer Ole Evinrude, who was building gas engines of his own design for automotive use on Milwaukee's Lake Street. The prototype of the new loop-frame Harley-Davidson was assembled in a small shed in the Davidson family back-yard. The new prototype was functional by September 8, 1904.

Harley-Davidson continued to make changes and improvements to its motorcycles year after year. In 1917 the United States entered World

War I and the military demanded motorcycles for the war effort. Harleys had already been used by the military in the Pancho Villa Expedition, but World War I was the first time the motorcycle had been adapted for combat service. Harley-Davidson provided about 15,000 machines to the military forces during World War I. By 1920, the company was the largest motorcycle manufacturer in the world, with 28,189 machines produced and dealers in sixty-seven countries. In 1921, a Harley-Davidson, rode by Otto Walker, was the first motorcycle ever to win a race at an average speed greater than 100 miles per hour.

In 1969, Harley-Davidson was sold to American Machine and Foundry (AMF), which streamlined production and slashed the workforce, resulting in a labor strike and a lower quality of motorcycle. Under AMF the motorcycles were expensive and inferior in performance, handling, and quality to competitive Japanese motorcycles. Sales and quality declined and the company almost went bankrupt. The Harley-Davidson name was mocked as Hardly Ableson, Hardly Drivable, and Hogly Ferguson, and the nickname "Hog" became a derogatory term.

In 1981, AMF sold the company to a group of thirteen investors led by Vaughn Beals and Willie G. Davidson for $80 million. In the early 1980s HD claimed that Japanese manufacturers were importing motorcycles into the United States in such volume as to harm or threaten to harm domestic producers. After an investigation by the US International Trade Commission, President Ronald Reagan imposed in 1983 a 45 percent tariff on imported bikes with engine capacities greater than 700 cubic centimeters. HD subsequently rejected offers of assistance from Japanese motorcycle makers. However, the company did offer to drop the request for the tariff in exchange for loan guarantees from the Japanese.

Rather than trying to match the Japanese motorcycles, the new management deliberately exploited the "retro" appeal of the HD machines, building motorcycles that deliberately adopted the look and feel of its earlier machines and the subsequent customizations of HD owners of that era. Many components such as brakes, forks, shocks, carburetors, electronics, and wheels were outsourced from foreign manufacturers, and quality increased. Technical improvements were made, quality improved, and buyers slowly returned.

After learning a valuable lesson in doing it right, Harley-Davidson continued to make substantial improvements to its motorcycles and brand; the company sustains a large brand community that keeps active through motorcycle clubs, scheduled rides and events, and a museum. Licensing of the Harley-Davidson brand and logo accounted for $40 million of the company's net revenue in 2010. As of 2011, Harley-Davidson employed six thousand workers and had sales in excess of $5.3 billion and total assets of nearly $10 billion. Today Harley-Davidson is truly an American success story. As an avid Harley owner, rider, and enthusiast myself, I am very happy that HD understands and lives by the do it right motto.

Do not be satisfied with average performance. Strive for excellence. If you cannot give your customers a better value and a better product, don't sell the product.
—*Alex Manoogian*

Apple learned a valuable lesson in doing it right. In 1974 Steve Jobs took a position as a video game designer with Atari. Several months later he left Atari to travel the world. At the age of twenty-one, with friend Steve Wozniak, Jobs cofounded Apple computers in his family's garage using capital they earned from selling Jobs's Volkswagen bus and Wozniak's scientific calculator. Together they revolutionized the computer industry by democratizing the technology and making the machines smaller, cheaper, more intuitive, and accessible to everyday customers. In 1980 Apple became publicly traded, with a market value of $1.2 billion on its very first day of trading. Jobs turned to marketing expert John Scully of Pepsi-Cola to be Apple's president. The next several products from Apple suffered significant design flaws resulting in recalls and consumer disappointment. Soon IBM surpassed Apple sales.

Scully believed that Jobs was hurting Apple, and executives began to faze him out. Jobs went on to purchase Pixar Animation Studios from George Lucas; the studio merged with the Disney Company in 2006, making Jobs the largest shareholder. Jobs returned to Apple in 1997, and revitalized the company with a new management team, altered stock options, and a self-imposed one dollar annual salary. Jobs did it right; he put Apple back on track and once again earned the attention of his customers.

Be a professional, be respectful; do it right. Be a professional in all aspects of life and in everything you do. Be a professional not just part of the time but all of the time. Assume that everyone you come into contact with is a future in-law or your next customer. Treat everyone with respect, use good manners all of the time.

Imagine this predicament: you're on your way to a very important job interview or a meeting with a new client, or to meet your fiancé's mother for the first time; you're running a little behind so you are driving a little faster than you should be, then all of the sudden someone cuts you off in traffic (intentionally or accidentally—it makes no difference); in haste you make a stupid comment or an immature gesture of aggravation to the driver who cut you off. You show up at your meeting, and everything seems to be going well. Then, midway through the meeting, you realize that the person who cut you off—the person you were less than professional or courteous too in traffic—is none other than the assistant to the person you are meeting with; that assistant was also running late. Or worse yet, the person to whom you were discourteous on the road is your future mother-in-law, who was herself running late and was having trouble finding the restaurant she was supposed to meet you and your fiancé at. The moral of this scenario is that you never know who you're coming in contact with; the world is much smaller than it seems, and you are likely to come into contact with the same people multiple times in your life; you should thus always treat everyone with courtesy and respect.

I was once called out to a large church in the middle of the night by one of my insurance adjuster clients. The church was in a very affluent area and had just suffered a terrible fire and was severely damaged. I showed up with some of my construction crew to assess the damages while they were performing some emergency services and securing the building. When I arrived, there was a couple of the church employees there trying to assist in securing the building; one would have easily assumed by their appearance and the work that they were doing that they were the church maintenance men or custodians. Fortunately for us we jumped right in and worked right beside them, and treated them like they were members of our own team. The next day I had a meeting at the church with the insurance adjuster and the head pastor of the church. The pastor was dressed in a suit, and I hardly recognized that he was none other than one of the men who was working right beside us the night before but had never introduced himself as the church pastor. Fortunately, we had treated him with great respect, and we earned their business. It just goes to show that you never know for sure who you are talking too, so treat everyone as if they are your next best customer.

Never burn a bridge for any reason. If you leave a job, do it right; do so on good terms, give your employer plenty of notice, and make sure that he or she knows to call you at any time in the future if you can ever be of any assistance. If you get laid off, understand that it's your employer's responsibility to do what he or she thinks is best for their business, and cutting payroll is often a very responsible necessity; don't take it personally. If you get fired, take it as a lesson, that for some reason you didn't live up to your employers expectations, accept it, learn from it, and move on. You will soon find out that every industry is relatively small, and if you are in it long enough you will sooner or later come full circle and run into people again and again. You will surely at some point want your former employer to speak highly of you; even if for some reason you leave on bad terms, be the bigger person.

If you are an employer or manager and are letting someone go—firing them or laying them off—be professional, but keep it short and to the point. Never let yourself be dragged into a debate about why you are letting him or her go; it won't change anything and it won't make either of you feel any better. My classic line was always, "I'm not sure how we're going to get along without you, but from this point forward, we are going to try." If the employee persists in trying to explain him- or herself, I would suggest ten simple words to remember: "I'm sorry you feel that way; I wish you well." If you end a friendship or romantic relationship, do so on good terms, even if the other person isn't willing to do so. Again, never let yourself be dragged in to any debate about why you don't want to be associated with someone any longer; is it really going to change anything or make anyone any happier? Does the *why* really matter, or does it only further the debate? Again, the ten simple words of wisdom to remember in such circumstances: "I'm sorry you feel that way, I wish you well." There is little response or comeback to that statement. You aren't arguing with others; you are acknowledging their feelings and letting them know that you wish them well. That ends the conversation, and doesn't invite any further debate.

You're a professional, so dress like a professional. There is no such thing as business casual. Assume that you are always meeting future employers or customers. Dress like you respect yourself, and dress like you respect the people you come in contact with on a daily basis. Keep yourself groomed properly at all times. You can only make one first impression; the problem is, you almost never know at what day or what time of day you will be making that first impression. If you knew you were going for that big job interview, or if you knew you were having lunch with a big potential client, or if you knew you were going to meet your future spouse for the first time; how would you want to present yourself? The rule of thumb is that you can never be overdressed, and you can easily be underdressed. If you are in sales or in business, and meeting clients and customers, jeans and pullover shirts are usually not acceptable attire. For men, dress slacks, dress shoes, and a collared button-down shirt, with a tie and jacket always on hand, keeps you ready for all situations. For women, dress should be professional, classy, and somewhat conservative—never provocative.

Always maintain a positive image and a positive attitude; these can get you a long way in life. If you have a positive image outlook, they will reflect in everything you do. People will be drawn to you, because anything positive is like sunlight, and people are naturally drawn to sunlight. If you have a negative image of yourself, and a negative outlook, well, who wants to be around that? Nobody. Be an optimist, not a pessimist; the glass is of course always half full, and an optimist is always going to keep adding to the glass to make sure that it is never close to being empty.

Anything worth doing is worth doing right; be the expert! Be the "go-to" person in your field or your industry. Choose a career or business that you enjoy and get a lot more satisfaction out of then just collecting a paycheck. If you enjoy what you are doing, it's easy to become an expert at it. Attend every class or seminar you can in your field, and obtain every certification you can. Being an expert gives you credibility, and credibility is a very marketable commodity. If you aren't earning as much as you would like, ask yourself if you are an expert in your field; if not, you need to either become an expert or change careers. If you are an expert at what you do, you will be confident at what you do, and confidence is a very admirable and marketable quality in someone.

When I founded the Horny Toad entertainment complex in the Lake of the Ozarks region in Missouri, one of my objectives was to provide outstanding entertainment to all of my patrons. Most of the other waterfront restaurants and bars had long been having live entertainment, mostly local and some regional bands from Kansas City, St. Louis, and the region. My objective was to do it right and eclipse that level of entertainment. Having grown up in the 1970s and early '80 s I had a real love for classic rock and roll, and having always been a cowboy at heart, I had a real passion for country music as well. I thought it would be great if I could build a state-of-the-art outdoor amphitheater and promote some of the greatest bands that I grew up on. That's exactly what I did; for a period of ten years I promoted over a hundred concerts, with legendary recording artists such as Willie Nelson, the Beach Boys, Uncle Kracker, Bret Michaels, Styx, the Steve Miller Band, REO Speed Wagon, Randy Travis, the Marshall Tucker Band, the Charlie Daniels Band, the Little River Band, and many, many more. It was truly fantastic getting to know some of the bands that I idolized growing up and providing my customers the very best entertainment possible. We definitely did our entertainment right, and it made my business a tremendous success. I immediately recognized the value of our concert series, and quickly realized that this was not only a great idea for my business but that it also afforded me the opportunity to raise money for a very worthwhile charity. I had previously been on the board of the YMCA, and, my construction company had designed and built the local Tri-County YMCA facility, thus making the YMCA a natural partner for these events. That relationship lead to a partnership with the Kiwanis Club, which raised money for the YMCA as well as several other children's charities. This made a perfect fit for my benefit concert series, and the Kiwanis children's charities became the beneficiary of all the net proceeds generated from our concerts for nearly a decade. Tying our concert series into a great local charity made my patrons feel good about buying a ticket to attend these incredible concerts, since all of the proceeds were going to a good cause; and in turn my business ended up with some fantastic entertainment at a reasonable cost.

If there should have been another chapter in this book—or, should I say, if there is another rule to success—it would be to give back, or, as they say, to "pay it forward." I learned several years ago the benefits of giving back. My construction and restoration company had built its success off rebuilding after natural disasters; so who better to build a charitable alliance with than the American Red Cross? My construction company profited off of disasters, but we made it a priority to give back to the victims of natural disasters through our charitable partnership with the Red Cross.

I truly believe that part of doing your business right, and even living your life right, means giving back in some meaningful way. It might be through your church, or any number of good charities, or even through volunteering your time or in mentoring other people you can have a positive influence on. If you have something to be thankful for, and something to offer, you owe it to yourself, the society, and humankind to pay it forward.

Not being satisfied with just offering my patrons the best live music available, I next set my sights on bringing the Offshore Super Series National Championship Power Boat Races to the Lake of the Ozarks, with the race course on the waters directly in front of my resort and entertainment complex. This took some real effort and great cost. I hooked up with a couple of my friends to help me get this endeavor off the ground; first my good buddy Dave Scott, six-time Offshore World Champion Power Boat Racer, and our mutual friend August Busch, CEO of Anheuser-Busch. I also hooked up with another longtime friend, Dave Leathers, who is the publisher of several quality magazines; several other friends, advertisers, and business associates joined us, all of whom were enthusiastic about being a part of such a fantastic event. These were not just any races; they were the national championships, just prior to the world championships in Key West, Florida! I've always been a huge boating enthusiast and love offshore racing; this was an event that I truly enjoyed. That work paid off big time! The finest racers came from all over the world, in multimillion-dollar boats that reached speeds upward of 200 miles per hour. It was not only a huge success for me and my business but also the largest single economic event that ever hit the Lake of the Ozarks, generating tens of millions of dollars for our local economy. It was a big home run, and we definitely did it right.

One good thing leads to another: the massive success of our benefit concert series and the National Championship Power Boat Races made me determined to create another incredible event for my business and our community. The Lake of the Ozarks has some of the most scenic landscape in the country; why not a great motorcycle rally? It's done wonders for Sturgis, South Dakota, and a great number of other communities, so why not the Lake of the Ozarks? I'm an avid motorcycle enthusiast and have been riding all my life; this made this event a perfect fit for me. Again, I called in some people I knew who could help make this event a reality; I no doubt tapped my great relationship with our local Budweiser distributor, and Anheuser-Busch, as well as *Full Throttle* motorcycle magazine and a couple of other successful local bar and restaurant owners. We all worked together, we did it right, and the event was a huge success and is still ongoing today.

All of these events that I've had a great deal of success with are a testament to the idea that if you enjoy something and you're passionate about it, doing your homework, planning it right, and executing it right are the keys to success. I've been very fortunate and very successful as an event promoter for over ten years because I networked with some really good people, and we did it right! Not only did we do it right, but we had a lot of fun at it, and made a lot of money at it.

Build it and they will come. That's only true if you build it right! I've spent over thirty years of my life building things, starting when I was a young boy building a three-story tree house. At the age of twenty-two, I designed and built my very first house from start to finish, by myself. I spent ten years of my life traveling the world rebuilding communities after natural disasters. I have built everything from large community centers to five-star resort hotels, to some of the finest multimillion-dollar mansions in the country. The one thing I learned at a very early age is that there is only one way to build something and that is to build it right! Starting with the right design, to the site work and foundation, and finishing with the landscaping, there is a right way to do everything, to ensure a successful and quality result. If you build it right, and build it with quality, there will always be a market for it. If you do it wrong, there is no point in doing it at all. Approach everything in life the same way you would approach building a house—or at least the same way you would want your contractor to build your house; do it right! What's the point in doing it wrong? Sooner or later it will come back around and bite you in the rear end. Those who think it's easier to do things on the cheap should think again. It never works out that way.

Building a good business is a lot like building a good house; you have to start with a good and viable plan—a road map or blueprint, as it were. Once you get your plan in place, you need to choose the right team; it's kind of like choosing the right contractor or subcontractors. Once you've designed your plan and chosen your team you can work on the foundation of your company, and what it is going to be built on. If you build your company right, build it with a good plan, the right people, a solid foundation, and a quality objective as your guiding principle, you are bound to end up with a successful outcome.

When building a quality business, it isn't good enough to simply be better than your competition; your customers likely don't know who your competition is, and you don't want them to know who your competition is. If you truly intend to build a quality and successful business, it's incumbent on you to be better than the businesses your customers do know about that aren't necessarily your competitors. I use the Disneyland comparison; your business has to be better than Disneyland. Your customer knows Disneyland and, like it or not, that is the standard you must aspire to meet. If you've been to Disneyland, you know what I'm talking about: everything is top shelf, top quality; the staff is friendly and professional, the entire park is always spotless and immaculate. The Disney hotels are among the finest in the world, and everything is always 100 percent consistent; that consistency is quality. If your customers aren't comparing you to their Disneyland experience, they are comparing you to their favorite quality restaurant or the UPS delivery guy who shows up at your front door in a nice clean truck, in a nice clean and professional uniform, hands you a package that you only ordered yesterday, is friendly, and quickly lets you get on with your day. Be better than your competition; you need to be as good as the highest-quality companies your customers have ever dealt with, because that is what their expectation is. Do it Right.

❯Action Steps

1. Identify the single most important thing that you are doing right in life.

2. Identify what it is that you think you may not be doing right in life but could be if you put forth the right effort.

3. Identify the single most important thing that you believe the company you own, manage, or work for does right.

4. Identify what it is that you think your company or the company that you manage or work for may not be doing right, but could be if you put forth the right effort.

5. Identify what your favorite restaurant or any other business you frequent does right.

The purpose of this exercise is to get you to think about and recognize what you and your business are already doing right and to focus on what you might not be doing right. Thinking about what other businesses you are familiar with do right can be beneficial when evaluating what it is that you could be doing better.

Write down your responses to these action steps before you move on to the next chapter.

CHAPTER FOUR

Keep Good Company

Surround yourself with good people. You are the captain of your ship; choose your crew cautiously and meticulously, or you will surely end up with a mutiny or two along your journey. Choose a crew that will help keep your ship afloat, will help keep you on the right course: a crew that can weather the storms and is loyal to the cause.

Before you can know who you should keep company with, you should first know yourself. What are your values? Values generally come down to four basic categories; self, God, society, and family. How do you feel about each of these? Self would include things like money, fame, respect, attitude, community standing, adventure, and fun. God would include things like life after death, performing your calling, and serving God or a higher purpose. Society would include things like helping those less fortunate and making the world a better place. Family would include things like providing resources for family survival, education, and happiness; how you raise your children; and leaving a legacy for your heirs.

Once you have acknowledged and understand your values, know your character. Be careful of your thoughts, for they become your words. Be careful of your words, for they become your actions. Be careful of your actions, for they become your habits. Be careful of your habits, for they become your character. Be careful of your character, for it becomes your destiny!

Define yourself; don't be defined by others. Know who you are, what you believe, and what is important to you. Be a leader, not a follower. Stand on your own two feet, and stand tall. Once you have a good handle on this, build your circle of friends, family, and associates based on your values and your character.

Start with a good first mate—your spouse, your soul mate, your partner in life. Choosing the person you may spend the rest of your life with is likely the most important decision you will ever make. Unfortunately, many people don't give much more serious consideration to whom they marry than they do when they buy a new car; when they are smitten with hormones and wedding bells ringing in their heads, there's not much reasoning with them, and they can easily be led astray.

Never settle; your spouse is the person you want by your side in sickness and in health, the person you want to have a family with, the person you want to wake up next to every morning for the rest of your life; choose very carefully! The right spouse can make all of the positive difference in your life, and the wrong person can completely suck all the life out of you and derail every goal or aspiration you have.

If you are in a relationship or married, and in love with your significant other, give that person and the relationship all you can give; never take it for granted. If you are in a toxic relationship or marriage that's beyond mending, cut your losses as quickly as possible and get on with your life. A bad marriage or a toxic relationship can be a cancer on you, your career, your business, and everyone around you.

You don't have to look far to realize the cost and devastating toll of a marriage gone wrong; the tabloids and reality television are loaded with celebrity divorces that cost a bundle and should make everyone take pause. When actor Kelsey Grammer divorced his wife Camille, one of the stars of *The Real Housewives of Beverly Hills*, it set him back a cool $50 million. That was only half of what it cost Steven Spielberg to divorce his wife of four years, actress Amy Irving; the couple did have a prenuptial agreement, but the judge refused to honor it because it was written on the back of a napkin, and awarded Irving a whopping $100 million. Before they married in 1985, Spielberg and Irving had dated in the late 1970s, but she had then dumped him for singer-songwriter Willie Nelson (that probably should have set the alarm bells off). Spielberg's $100 million divorce settlement is chump change compared to the $750 million dollars that golfing legend Tiger Woods had to cough up to his wife of six years, Elin Nordegren, after his numerous extramarital affairs became public knowledge. And that wasn't the worst of it for Woods; he also lost millions if not billions more in future endorsements, his professional game took a serious hit, and his once very marketable Tiger Woods brand will never be the same. Don't get me wrong; I'm not suggesting that all of these spouses didn't deserve whatever settlement they received. What I am suggesting is that if these people knew in foresight what they soon found out in hindsight, they might have made some very different decisions and might have conducted themselves in a much different manner. Or possibly not; Kelsey Grammer has since remarried, and reportedly again chose not to have a prenuptial agreement, which either makes him a hopeless romantic or a glutton for punishment (probably the latter).

If it seems like I often refer to relationships and marriages throughout this book, I do so for good reason. There is probably no more important decision that you will ever make in your life than that of who you want to spend the rest of your life with. The right person can have a tremendously positive impact on your life and your future, and the wrong person can have the single most detrimental impact on your life, your career, your business, and your future.

How about your friends? Who are your friends? Are they a positive influence on you? Do they have the same goals, ideals, and character as you, or are they going no place fast and trying to take you down with them? Misery loves company.

Soar with the eagles, don't run with the turkeys. Surrounding yourself with good and positive people is bound to have a positive reflection on you and your life. Surrounding yourself with losers, criminals, or people without any ambition is bound to have a bad influence on your life.

Take a long hard look at all the people you have in your life. Make a serious assessment of who gives you positive encouragement and who sucks the life right out of you. Then make a conscious decision to put your effort into the friendships and relationships that you get something positive out of and distance yourself from the people who are sucking the life out of you. Surround yourself with people you enjoy communicating with, people who have similar goals and aspirations, people who expect nothing but friendship and give as much as they get.

One of my good friends in both my personal life and my business life, is August Busch IV, former CEO of Anheuser-Busch (AB), who was at the helm of the company in November of 2008, during the company's hostile takeover by the Belgian-Brazilian beer company InBev. The takeover was a double-edged sword. On one end was the end of a family legacy that began back in 1860, and the end of an American business Icon. Anheuser-Busch had long been the largest beer company in America, demanding over 49 percent of the entire U.S. market share. Timing was everything; AB had not established itself nearly as dominantly on the international stage as it had in the United States, making it somewhat vulnerable to a foreign takeover; combine that with the global economic collapse that occurred in the third quarter of 2008, which made AB prime pickings. The other edge of the sword, however, is that AB was able to push the price of its stock to $70 per share, which generated $52 billion for the company, making most of its stockholders very happy. After all, the hard truth is that the primary responsibility of any CEO is to his stockholders. My friend August took a lot of hits from all directions about the takeover of the largest American beer company, and of the end of his family's legacy; but at the end of the day, the deal made his stockholders a lot of money. And as CEO that was his primary responsibility.

August and I met in the late 1990s shortly after I opened the Horny Toad Entertainment Complex in Missouri's Lake of the Ozarks. I first met his dad, August III, who used to come into my restaurant for lunch once in a while. In a couple of years, the Horny Toad grew to be one of Anheuser-Busch's largest on-premise accounts in the United States. We would regularly sell over a thousand cases of Bud Light alone on any given summer weekend. Our AB distributor, Missouri Eagle, took notice of our growing business right away, and it didn't take long for Anheuser-Busch to take notice of our business from their St. Louis headquarters. Being St. Louis natives, the Busch family spent a lot of time at the Lake of the Ozarks. August IV and I are pretty close to the same age, and have a lot in common; he obviously came from a background much different from mine, but we both had a real appreciation for the lake and a zeal for life, and we were both in the beer business. It didn't take either of us long to realize that we had a lot to offer each other in our friendship. August and I provided a great sounding board for one another in a business that was hard for both of us to get open-minded council that would tell us what we needed to hear and not just what we wanted to hear. A real friend will tell you what you need to hear and sometimes what you don't want to hear.

In life you have what I call three circles of friends and associates. First you have your inner circle: your closest family, advisers, and friends. Next you have your secondary circle, which comprises extended family, friends, and associates that you would consider friends but are not the kind of friends that you could call in the middle of the night and borrow a thousand dollars from if you were in a bad spot. These are friends that you might work with or do business with, but probably wouldn't go on vacation with. Then you have your outer circle of friends; these might be some of your customers that you don't deal with on a regular basis but you know who they are. It might be the guy at the dry cleaning shop, or the barber or stylist who does your hair; you have a good but cordial relationship but probably don't even know these people's last names.

Choose your inner circle of friends and associates very carefully, as these are the people who usually have unfettered access to you, and you to them; these are the people who may provide a lot of influence.

At the end of 2013 there were over 320 million people in the United States, and about 7.2 billion people in the world, with the world population increasing by nearly 80 million people every year. That's a whole heck of a lot of people! My point is that there are a whole lot of people to choose to be friends with in life, so you can afford to be very picky! Your inner circle of friends needs to be only a small handful of people, probably not more than five or ten individuals, so chose them wisely—you can't afford not to. In choosing your inner circle, have zero tolerance for bat-shit crazy. Avoid it at all costs, and if it's already in your inner circle, get rid of it. Don't laugh—you know what I'm talking about!

Honesty, dependability, and loyalty: everyone in your inner circle should possess all of these qualities. I would add that they must also have a positive attitude. But honesty, dependability, and loyalty are not qualities you can usually teach people. They are part of their character; people either have these qualities or they don't, they either are, or are not instilled in them at a very early age. It's not that someone with a tremendous amount of soul searching and effort can't improve on these attributes and overcome character flaws; however they would first need to acknowledge their shortcomings, and undertake serious efforts to overcome them. For me, lack of these three qualities is a deal killer; I don't want to be friends with anyone who doesn't possess all three, and

I certainly don't want anyone working for my businesses who doesn't possess all three.

Surround yourself with people who are smarter than you are and draw from their knowledge and experiences. Surround yourself with people who inspire you, and support your plan to be all you can be. Choose friends who have the same interests as you and have good morals, and preferably those involved in the same or a similar industry you are in or wish to be in. Ambition should be a prerequisite. Surround yourself with people who are honest, dependable, loyal, motivated, goal-oriented, of good character, have a positive attitude, and want a lot out of life.

It is also important for you to be a part of your inner circle's inner circle. In other words, once you know who comprises your inner circle, ask yourself if you are also part of those people's inner circles. And if not, ask yourself why not. If you are going to be able to count on and depend on those in your inner circle, it is also important for them to be able to depend on and count on you. No good friendship or relationship should ever be a one-way street. Give as much as you get, and get as much as you give.

Networking is the best way to market yourself and your business; it is also a great way to cultivate friendships with like-minded people. There are a limitless number of networking opportunities in every community and in every industry. Join industry or trade organizations and become actively involved in as many as you can. Join the Rotary Club and your local or regional chamber of commerce (both can provide excellent marketing opportunities), as well as any other civic organizations you have access to in your community. If you attend church, that can also be a good place to network and for meeting people with similar beliefs and interests.

Partnerships are usually tough on all levels and often end in bitter lawsuits and hard feelings; there is usually one person who's the rainmaker, one who carries the bulk of the load, and another who simply hangs on to the others' shirttails. Partnerships are kind of like marriages, and like marriages, at least half of them don't work out. Don't get me wrong; there are a lot of good partnerships, but they are generally the exception and not the rule.

Eduardo Saverin knows a thing or two about partnerships, and unfortunately learned the hard way. No doubt he surrounded himself with people as smart or even smarter than he is, and he certainly surrounded himself with people with high ambitions. Their ethics and scruples may have been in question however. Saverin was college roommates with Mark Zuckerberg when they cofounded Facebook in 2004. Saverin wasn't only one of the cofounders, he was the original financier that got the company started. The two literally started the company in their dorm room at Harvard University, and Facebook went on to become a world-wide phenomenon. Reportedly Zuckerberg and his new investors pushed Saverin out of the company; resulting in a bitter lawsuit between the once best friends. The ending isn't all bad, however, depending on how you look at it. This partnership and business endeavor definitely severed their friendship, and Saverin probably, justifiably feels like he ended up getting the short end of the stick. That said, his friendship and partnership with Zuckerberg made him a billionaire at a very young age. Today Zuckerberg is one of the wealthiest men in America, and Facebook is a true American success story. The Facebook story doesn't end there, however; two other Harvard classmates who also considered themselves business partners with Zuckerberg definitely feel like they got the short end of the stick. Twin brothers Cameron and Tyler Winklevoss accused Zuckerberg of intentionally misleading them and stealing their social networking idea. The dispute ended in a high-profile lawsuit that dragged on in court for nearly seven years. Facebook went public in 2012, and after a rocky first year, by September of 2013 the company stock was valued at over $100 billion! Not bad for a company that started in a college dorm room only seven years earlier. The moral of the story is to choose your friends wisely, and to choose your business partners even more wisely.

Another case of someone who might have chosen the wrong partner is mild mannered Jack Dorsey, who founded Twitter in 2006. According to a Dorsey profile in *Vanity Fair* magazine, cofounder Evan Williams and the Twitter board forced Dorsey out of his position as CEO. Dorsey still remained chairman of Twitter after the turmoil, but the two reportedly rarely speak anymore. That said, there was nonetheless obviously some sort of chemistry between Dorsey and Williams that made things happen at one point; Twitter is a huge American business success story.

Las Vegas magnate Stephen Wynn was on the rebound after his casino and resort empire Mirage Resorts was sold after an unsolicited takeover in 2000. Japanese billionaire Kazuo Okada bankrolled his comeback, and together they formed Wynn Resorts, with Okada eventually becoming the company's biggest shareholder.

"I love Kazuo Okada as much as any man that I've ever met in my life," Wynn said during an earnings conference call in May 2008, as reported by the *New York Times*. Well, that love affair is now over; Wynn and Okada ended up embroiled in one of the worse public feuds that the international resort industry has ever seen, with each accusing the other of questionable payments to public officials in Asia. It was like two gunslingers shooting it out, said a longtime industry official, who insisted on anonymity because he knew both men and wanted to protect his relationship with each.

Partnerships with friends can be difficult enough, but partnerships with family can lead to a whole different realm of difficulty and can cause a significant wedge between families—possibly even a dagger. Brothers Adolf and Rudolf Dassler founded a shoe company in their mother's laundry room back in 1924. Because they had distinctly different personalities, the partnership soon resulted in major tension. Rudolf was imprisoned after his return from World War II and was convinced that his brother was behind his incarceration. The two parted ways in 1948, and Rudolf went on to become the founder of Puma. His brother

Adi went on to be the founder of Adidas. The bitter rivalry between the two brothers even divided their entire hometown of Herzogenaurach, Germany, where Adidas and Puma still have rival factories on opposite sides of the river.

Brothers Jimmy and Larry Flint cofounded *Hustler* magazine—or did they? According to Jimmy Flint, *Hustler* belongs to him every bit as much as to his more famous brother Larry. However, Larry claims that Jimmy was never anything more than an employee, and not a very good one at that. This family feud boiled over and came to a head when Larry fired Jimmy's two sons, severed ties with his brother, and tried to have him evicted from a Hustler store he ran in Cincinnati.

I've had a great deal of experience with family members working for me in the past, and I can tell you firsthand that it can be a challenge. I've had most of the people in my family work for me at one time or another: my father, my son, my daughter, my sister, my stepbrother, my brother-in-law, my sister-in-law, my nieces, and my nephews. Don't get me wrong, there are times that it can be very rewarding; my father worked for me for about eight years, and even though there were a few testy times, I think we both greatly appreciated and enjoyed it. That unfortunately is more likely the exception than the rule; working with family is far more likely to cause family problems than not, and there is nothing worth causing problems between you and the ones you love. I would suggest you think long and hard about doing business with family; the problems are likely to far outweigh the benefits.

Choose a great team of professional counselors: attorneys, accountants, insurance agents, and business coaches. These professionals can mean the difference between success and failure or even between life and death. Chose professionals whom you not only trust but also get along well with. Put a lot of effort into choosing these individuals, and develop a productive and mutually beneficial long-term relationship.

They should be an intricate part of your inner circle, and they are all likely to become your most trusted advisers.

Align yourself with good legal counsel. Depending on the extent to which you are involved in business, you will likely need several different attorneys; in any event, you will need one good business attorney to be your legal quarterback, so to speak. Understand that attorneys are like doctors: they often have specific areas of law that they practice and specialize in. Just as you wouldn't want a dentist doing open heart surgery, you probably wouldn't want a trust or contract attorney doing litigation for you. Choose an attorney who specializes in what your specific legal needs are, and don't expect miracles; do as much of the heavy lifting yourself as possible. Attorneys aren't mind readers, and likely know far less than you do about the case you want them to represent you in; so put forth an effort to assist them however you can; it will save you lots of money and greatly increase the chances of a successful outcome.

A good certified public accountant (CPA) is a must for anyone—especially anyone who is in business for him- or herself. Make sure that your accountant specializes in your business. Though most accountants have a pretty broad understanding of businesses, they too are much like doctors and lawyers in that many accountants have specific areas of expertise. If your CPA doesn't exactly specialize in your business, make sure he or she *becomes* a specialist in your industry and business. Make sure that your accountant knows everything about your financial portfolio and all of your income and expenses; seek out your CPA's advice on how to maximize your earnings and best limit your tax liabilities. Keep in mind that CPAs aren't mind readers either; they will only know what you tell them. Have your accountant teach you everything he or she can about accounting and how it affects you and your business. Your CPA will most likely become part of your inner circle.

If you have any assets at all, you'd better have them insured. If you have a family, you'd better have yourself insured. A good and qualified insurance agent can help you assess your risks and protect you from loss. Insurance agents also specialize in certain forms of insurance and coverage; you may need two or three agents to cover such different risks as life, health, property, auto, and business. Your insurance agent might or might not become part of your inner circle but would certainly become part of your secondary circle.

If you are in business for yourself, or are planning on going into business for yourself, a professional business coach can be an extremely valuable resource. A good business coach can help you navigate through the pitfalls and give you experienced guidance in determining risks versus rewards. Most entrepreneurs find it difficult to find other successful businesspeople to discuss problems and ideas with, and getting advice from the wrong people can be much worse than getting no advice at all. A good business coach can provide that much-needed sounding board to bounce ideas off and get an informed opinion. If a good business coach doesn't have all the answers, he or she will likely have the resources to find you the answers. You need someone who will tell you what you need to know, and often what you don't want to hear; a good business coach can provide that guidance. Most people and most business owners usually know the answers to their challenges; the problem is that they forget what questions they should be asking themselves. A professional business coach can help you ask yourself the right questions.

Business owners must be particularly aware of the company they keep. The people you hire are a direct reflection of the business and the business owner; hiring the wrong ones can be detrimental to your business and your livelihood. I hate to be cynical, but not everyone is honest, and sometimes even people who might be fairly honest under normal circumstances aren't always completely honest to their employer. They may not even think of it as being dishonest; maybe they cheat on their time card, and don't even think of it as stealing. Being in the restaurant business for as many years as I have been, I often had issues with bartenders buying people drinks (which means that I bought the drinks) or not charging them full price or for all of their drinks, in exchange for larger tips; this too is obviously stealing. Then there is the excuse that some employees use to justify stealing; they think they are owed it for some reason: I work harder than everyone else, I'm not paid enough, or my boss doesn't appreciate me, and so on. There's no doubt that when you are in business for yourself you can't afford *not* to keep good company.

Having been in the general contracting business my whole life, I know about this all too well: estimators and/or project managers making promises that they can't or don't deliver on, or underestimating or mismanaging a project; the wrong manager can sink an entire company in a hurry. Not to mention the project manager who's doing side jobs of his own behind the company's back, and even charging for materials for those jobs on employers' accounts, or worse yet stealing entire jobs from the company. Then there are the subcontractors who either don't do what they say they are going to do when they say they are going to do it; or subcontractors not paying their suppliers, resulting in liens filed against customers' properties. Then there is the downright unscrupulous subcontractor who agrees to do a project for one price, and tries billing more than the agreed amount for no good reason and without authorization. I'm here to tell you it happens all the time. Don't get me wrong, there are a lot of fantastic construction professionals out there, and some equally dynamic subcontractors; the key is making sure that the people you are working with are quality individuals and run quality businesses. That usually means that they aren't going to be the cheapest, and if they are the cheapest, that should ring some warning alarms. Surrounding yourself with good people can easily be the key to the success of any business; the wrong people can be a major nightmare. Keep good company!

Most of us have this inner radar that tells us who is healthy to have in our lives and who we should avoid. Unfortunately, we don't always listen to that inner radar, or that gut feeling. I suppose its human nature for us to want to help those around us to become better people, or make excuses as to why some people are the way they are. Unless the people in need are your immediate family members, or you're a psychiatrist and those people are your patients, it's not your job to try and fix or help everyone. OK, give people a hand up, but if and only if they are willing to do the heavy lifting for themselves and you have your feet firmly planted on the ground; but the second you feel yourself being pulled toward the black hole, it's time to cut loose and not look back. This is the same basic instinct we have as parents, and most of our parents had when we were kids. As a parent you instinctively know who your kids should or shouldn't be hanging out with, even though sometimes your kids never see it themselves. As a parent you would do most anything to keep your kids safe and keep them from hanging out with the wrong people. Unfortunately, as adults, that same instinct about who we let into our lives sometimes gets clouded.

Keep good company! This is an important enough topic to have deserved its own chapter, because the people immediately around us have such a huge influence on our lives, our careers, and our businesses. These people can provide an extremely positive influence on our lives or they can be a terminal cancer to us. This is also something that everyone can take immediate action to change in his or her life if need be.

❭Action Steps

1. Make a careful assessment of the people in your life; ask yourself the hard question of whether each of those people is a good influence on you, if each supports your goals, dreams, and aspirations wholeheartedly.

2. Identify anyone in your life who is a bad influence on you, is holding you back from accomplishing your dreams, or is sucking the life out of you; distance yourself from that individual immediately.

3. Identify your inner circle of close friends and family; ask yourself if you get as much as you give from them, and if you give as much as you get from them; if not, ask yourself why.

The people you surround yourself with have a lot of influence on your life; make sure that that influence is positive and healthy. If you don't take any other step that is recommended in this book, take this step: surround yourself with good people. Keep good company.

Write down the people you would relate these action steps to before you move on to the next chapter; then once you've finished this book, take the necessary action to surround yourself with good people, and limit your exposure to the people who may not be such a good influence in your life.

CHAPTER FIVE

Be a Rainmaker

American tradition defines a rainmaker as "one who makes it rain" to nourish the lands and support the people. *Merriam-Webster's Collegiate Dictionary* defines a rainmaker as "a person who produces or attempts to produce rain by artificial means" or—more important for our discussion here—"a person (as a partner in a law firm) who brings in new business" and "a person whose influence can initiate progress or ensure success." In modern business, *rain* is a synonym for *money*! In business, a rainmaker is a money-maker. A make-it-happen person isn't always necessarily a rainmaker, but a rainmaker is *always* a make-it-happen person. The first step in being a rainmaker is to take action, and make it happen.

As the captain of your ship, you had better be a rainmaker, or at least make sure that you have a good rainmaker or two on your crew; if your journey is worthwhile it's going to take adequate financial resources to reach your destiny, so you had better make sure you have the ability to meet those financial demands and obligations. If not, your ship will surely run out of steam, and you will likely be left adrift and looking for a life raft.

Not everyone has this talent or ability, but that doesn't mean that it can't be cultivated if one has the right personality, and confidence. But if you are lacking in confidence and the right personality they are difficult if not impossible to cultivate. Not everyone can be a rainmaker—in fact, damn few ever are. If you are a really good rainmaker— if you are disciplined and can master the talent—you will likely be very successful and have the ability to make a great deal of money in your life. Maybe you don't have the personality to be a rainmaker in business, but everyone should at the very least be a rainmaker in his or her own life.

Rainmakers understand that they are part of what makes a business work, that they are part of or an extension of the management team. A rainmaker understands that there is no such thing as a forty-hour workweek and puts forth whatever effort and hours are necessary to make rain (money). Have you ever known people working in management who receive salaries for their work, and are constantly complaining about the hours they have to work, and even go so far as to break their salaries down to an hourly rate? I would suggest that those individuals need a bit of a reality check and should probably go out and get an hourly, mediocre, forty-hour-a-week job.

Many companies make a mistake early on by thinking that throwing lots of advertising at something will automatically result in sales. Smart and targeted advertising can be valuable, but I would rather have one good rainmaker over all the advertising in the world.

Regardless of what business you are in, all businesspeople are in the people business. People don't buy from businesses; people buy from people! A good rainmaker truly understands this idea and cultivates it. A rainmaker understands and thrives on networking, and never misses an opportunity to meet new people and cultivate new friendships and business relationships.

Advertising is a funny animal, and often not a good investment because it either is poorly produced, not effectively targeted at your customer, suffers a lack of adequate frequency, or does not carry a consistent message. Once a dollar of advertising is spent, it's spent and gone forever, and there is no getting it back. Never spend any dollars on "ego advertising"; in other words; don't spend money on advertising just because you want to hear your company's name on radio or television, or you think it's the "it" thing to be in one magazine or another, or you think it might be cool to be on the big billboard you pass on your way into work. Advertising is extremely expensive, and if you don't use it properly you are far better off not doing it at all. If you can't spend enough to make a difference, and if you don't have the right marketing plan, save your money.

I used to think that I had had my first lesson in salesmanship when I was nineteen years old and worked evenings and weekends selling Kirby vacuum cleaners from door to door. At the time I was making about $340 a week, swinging a hammer during the day, and I could almost double my income if I only sold one Kirby vacuum each week. Kirby is a great product, but if you could sell vacuum cleaners for a thousand dollars each in the early 1980s you could sell anything.

I said that I thought that I had my first lesson in salesmanship when I first started selling vacuum cleaners, but that isn't correct. My first lesson in selling anything was selling myself—not literally, but figuratively. When you are an adolescent, at some point you start noticing the opposite sex, and sooner or later you make your first sales pitch, when you ask someone to go on a date or to the prom. That is your first sales call. Some are too shy, and have to wait for someone to ask them out, and some get shot down and have a hard time ever bringing themselves back into the game.

I have hired a lot of salespeople in my life, and before I ever hire a salesperson I want to meet his or her significant other. You can laugh about that, but ask yourself who some of the best salespeople you know are, and I will just about guarantee you that their spouses or significant others are exceptional in some manner. They are either really attractive, really talented, or just genuinely delightful people to be around. No doubt, beauty is in the eye of the beholder, but if someone is a true rainmaker, a "closer," he or she is going to have high aspirations when choosing a spouse and is going to "close the deal." Trust me, if you manage or hire rainmakers, put this test in your pocket.

One of the most well-known rainmakers of modern time was Sam Walton, who began his lifelong career in the retail business in 1940 when he took a job as a salesman with J. C. Penney in Des Moines, Iowa. Walton wasn't what his managers considered the ideal employee because, like most rainmakers, he didn't like fussing with paperwork and wanted to spend all of his time with his customers. His district manager once told Walton, "I'd fire you if you weren't such a damn good salesman," At the age of twenty-seven Walton put up $5,000 of his own money, borrowed $20,000 from his father-in-law, and purchased a Ben Franklin general store in Newport, Arkansas. Walton opened Walton's Five and Dime in the summer of 1950, and by 1960 he owned fifteen stores but still wasn't seeing the profits he expected. He adopted a new strategy of big stores with drastically discounted prices that would undercut the competition. Mortgaging his home, and borrowing to the hilt, Walton was able to open the first Walmart in 1962 in Rogers, Arkansas. He first kept his growth far off the beaten path, in smaller rural communities, to avoid being crushed by larger retailers. Small-town America was thrilled to have big city discounting and flocked to Walmart. In 1985, Forbes magazine named Walton the wealthiest man in the United States. Walton died on April 5, 1992, at the age of seventy-four.

There is only one boss, the customer. And he can fire everybody in the company from the chairman on down, simply by spending his money somewhere else.
—Sam Walton

So what's the one single quality that a rainmaker must possess? Confidence—plain and simple. Confidence, personality, and a polished presentation will get it every time. Product knowledge is a good plus, but confidence and personality will beat out product knowledge every day of the week.

The rainmaker's credo is, "People buy from people, not businesses." It's about building relationships and listening to your customers. If you are a rainmaker, you must master the ability to determine who the decision makers are and make damn sure that is who you are dealing with. One of the biggest mistakes that a salesperson can make is not knowing or understanding who makes the decisions. Treat everyone as if he or she is the decision maker, but focus your attention on whomever the decision maker really is. If you have an appointment with a new client and meet at his or her office, never discount the front office staff members; one of them could likely be your potential client's spouse or significant other.

Monetize what you are selling to your customers: tell them and show them how your product makes or saves them money. Maybe your product costs more than that of your competition; explain why there is a price difference and how that difference is actually a cost savings in the long run. Let your customers know that once they compare apples to apples, your product is the better value. If you can't get a solid answer to that question down, you need to meet with your company and figure out why—or find another product to sell. People are very price conscience, especially given the current economic conditions; but service sells, and it is perceived as a real value to most clients.

A good rainmaker is always honest, and never oversells or under delivers. You are only as good as your word, and once you have broken your word to your customer you have lost that customer forever, and likely everyone else that your customer knows or does business with. Don't oversell your product or your abilities; establish realistic expectations. It is much preferable to have to explain why you can't meet an unrealistic deadline than to have to explain why you didn't meet your commitment. Always strive to achieve exceptional results; exceed your customer's expectations.

A good rainmaker always listens to the customer. Ask what you or your company or your products can do better; ask for your customers' objections; once you know their objections, you have narrowed down the obstacles you must overcome. Take this as a positive, not a negative. If you are getting an honest line of communication with your customers, that is half the battle.

Ask for your customers' advice, even if it is about something you may already know the answers to. People appreciate being asked for their advice; it shows them that you respect their opinions.

Listen to your customers, and don't bore them with the events of your life; they really do not care about the vacation you just had, or your new baby, or about your sick parents. On the same note, don't ask your customers questions that you don't care about or that have no relationship to your business at hand. Time is valuable; don't waste it. If you find yourself giving someone your résumé, it's time to shut up!

Ask questions, and assume nothing! The last question you should always ask your customer is what, if anything, did I miss? If it's appropriate, be sure to set up your next appointment.

A good rainmaker is never sick at sea and is never on vacation. Your customers don't care about you not feeling well, and don't care if you ever take a vacation. If you are unavailable, you are unavailable because you are taking care of business, taking care of another customer, in a meeting or a conference. If you ever answer your phone and are unable to talk at that time, it's always because you are taking care of another client or are in a meeting; that is something that your clients can relate to, and respect; they don't care about your personal issues, no matter what they say, and they certainly don't' want to think that your personal matters are more important than their business is.

A good rainmaker seldom ever makes cold calls; they are almost always a total waste of your time and your potential client's time. Figure out what you can do to help a potential customer that you want to do business with; then send that potential client a note or an e-mail that lets him or her know that you have something that would help their company make or save money, and request five minutes of his or her time; let the person know that if you don't hear back in the next day or so that you will follow up with a phone call. Then follow up and make the appointment. Two points you get across in your initial communications: (1) you have a way to save or make this person money, and (2) it won't take more than five minutes of his or her time to meet with you.

When you get to the appointment, cut to the chase; you are a busy professional, and the person you are trying to sell to is a busy professional. Make a compelling presentation, then get his or her business. If you are going to make small talk, do it only as you are leaving.

Once you have closed a deal and are halfway through whatever the process is of delivering on the sale, be thinking ahead and asking for the next sale. Think down the road: you have already earned a customer's business; now expand your expectations and expand the business. Never give away for nothing, something that you should be compensated for. Never forget to say thank you, and often.

Lunch is a good place to meet a client for a business appointment, and breakfast is an even better place. Keep in mind that you are not there to eat a meal; you are there to do business. Eat light and avoid alcohol, unless you are meeting for a beer after work; in that event, drink lightly, and never be intoxicated around your customers.

A good rainmaker always assumes he or she is making the sale, and never goes anyplace without a business card and—most important—a contract. Never ask a question that can be answered with a negative reply. Instead of asking if customers would like to buy one, ask if they would like to start with two units or three, and let them know that if they could use four units right now you can work them a better discount.

A good rainmaker always returns every phone call—at the end of each day if at all possible, but always within twenty-four hours.

Five things that are the kiss of death for a rainmaker:

1. A rainmaker *never* inquires about a new job for him- or herself with *any* of the company's customers or clients. This is a sure sign of weakness and disloyalty, which will only leave your customers with a bad taste in their mouths. Trust me, if you are a true rainmaker and are looking to make a change in your career, you will have no shortage of unsolicited offers.

2. A rainmaker *never* has anything derogatory to say to anyone about his or her employer or coworkers. If you need to vent, vent only to your spouse or close personal council, such as a business coach. If you don't like your employer, or your coworkers, work out your differences or find another job.

3. A rainmaker *never* has anything derogatory to say about the competition or the competition's products. A good rainmaker can tactfully show a customer why his or her product or service is better than that of the competition without saying anything negative.

4. A rainmaker *never* burns a bridge—not with a customer and not with an employer. The world is a relatively small place, and whatever industry you are in is relatively tiny. You will be amazed at the people you run into over and over again, not to mention all of the

people your employer or your clients know. It is far better to bite your tongue, part ways as amicably as possible, and move on.

5. A rainmaker *never* shows up to an appointment late! If you are not punctual, then you are not dependable, and successful businesspeople will not deal with people they can't depend on. If you make an agreement to meet someone and you show up ten minutes late, you have already broken the most simple of agreements you can make with someone, which was to be somewhere when you said you would. If you can't be trusted to show up on time, it is unlikely that you can be trusted to do anything else you agree to do.

It's much easier to keep a customer than it is to earn a customer. This is a terrible mistake that many businesses and salespersons quickly forget, but a rainmaker never forgets. Half of your marketing efforts and half of your advertising budget should be spent on your existing customers. A good rainmaker will cultivate those customers and network with them to create new customers. Never let your customer feel unappreciated, because—believe me—there are vultures lining up at the gate, ready to do whatever they can to steal your customers away; and if you aren't taking care of your customers, someone else certainly will. If you are taking good care of your customers; they will provide you all the business you can handle simply by referrals.

If you are going to be a bear, be a grizzly bear; if you are hunting, hunt big game. A good rainmaker spends a part of everyday trying to land the trophy buck or the big fish. If you are going to be successful you need to hunt where the big bucks run or fish where the big fish swim. Never waste any time scouting for business in fields that the big bucks don't frequent; what's the point?

A rainmaker is *always* dependable and punctual. Punctual means no less than a minute early. Time is the most valuable commodity there is; it is the one thing that you can't buy, no matter how much money you have, and it is the one thing that you can never get back once it's lost. Personally, I don't ever want to do business with anyone who is not punctual or that I can't depend on. Quite frankly, I don't really want to associate with or be friends with someone I can't depend on. If you are not a punctual person, you are not a dependable person. If you aren't dependable, you might consider doing some serious soul searching and figure out why, as it is a terrible character flaw that will plague your ability to reach success.

A rainmaker is always professional and courteous, never casual. A rainmaker dresses for success. It is hard to be overdressed, but it is easy to be underdressed. Business casual is the minimum in appropriate attire for a rainmaker. Good manners are a standard trademark for every rainmaker, as is treating everyone as a friend and potential client. Rainmakers do unto others as they wish and expect people to do unto them.

We can't talk about rainmakers without including Richard Branson's story. Branson struggled through his youth with dyslexia, which made school extremely difficult. At the age of sixteen, Branson dropped out of school and started selling records out of the trunk of his car; he also started a youth culture magazine called *Student*. The publication, run by students for students, sold $8,000 worth of advertising in its first edition alone, which was launched in 1966. The first magazine run included fifty thousand copies that were disseminated for free after Branson covered the costs with the advertising he had sold. In 1969, Branson was living in a London commune, surrounded by the British music and drug scene, and it was at that time that Branson had the idea to start up a mail-order record company called Virgin to help fund his magazine efforts. Branson soon opened a record shop on Oxford Street in London. The success of the record shop enabled the high school dropout to build a recording studio in 1972 in Oxfordshire, England. His first artist on the Virgin Records label was Mike Oldfield, with the hit single *Tubular Bells* in 1973. The song was an instant smash hit, and stayed on the UK charts for 247 weeks. With the momentum of that success, he went on to sign recording legends such as Genesis and the Rolling Stones, making Virgin Music one of the top six record companies in the world.

Branson also started multiple other businesses, His Virgin Group holds more than two hundred companies, including Virgin Atlantic Airways and, more recently, the space tourism company Virgin Galactic. Branson is also known for his adventurous spirit and sporting achievements. In 2013 Branson's net worth was estimated to be $4.6 billion, making him one of the most successful rainmakers of all time.

At the end of the day, the success of any business is dependent on sales. Sales cures all. A good rainmaker can make the difference between a business succeeding and failing. A good rainmaker is usually among the highest-paid person in any company, and for good reason; a company can't exist without sales, and a good rainmaker fuels sales.

At the very least, be a rainmaker in your own life. It is incumbent on you to be your own rainmaker, because no one else is going to do it for you. Learn how to sell yourself; that starts with building self-confidence. How do you build confidence? Knowledge, knowledge is confidence. When you know something well, you know your facts; then you know what you are talking about in a conversation, and that in and of itself displays confidence. Take care of yourself physically and mentally; that builds confidence. When you take care of yourself, you establish the ability to present yourself well, and that too displays confidence. Be dependable and punctual always. Say what you mean and mean what you say; and do what you say you are going to do. When people realize they can count on you, it establishes confidence, and that is a very marketable quality. These qualities are not rocket science; they are all qualities that people have within themselves. Rainmakers acknowledge these qualities, cultivate them, and make them part of their character. Be one such person and you will be amazed at the doors that will open up to you.

❯Action Steps

1. If you are in sales or own your own business, identify the best potential customer you don't already have, and go out and sell yourself to that customer.

2. If you are working for a company, demonstrate your value to your employer, and sell yourself to your employer to get the raise or promotion that you believe you deserve.

3. If you are single, ask someone out on a date this week.

4. If you are in a relationship, convince your significant other to do something out of the ordinary that you think you both would really enjoy.

5. Sell something of value that you own but no longer need or want. (Sell it through the newspaper, the Internet, a garage sale or any other venue you can think of.)

6. This is your most important action step yet: finish reading this book, and convince a friend or colleague to buy it and read it.

The first step in being a rainmaker, or at least a good salesperson is to first ask yourself the question of what it is you want. You will never get what you want out of life, or ever make a sale, if you don't know what you want, and ask for what you want. Ask for the sale.

Make a note of what you can now regarding these action steps, then once you have finished this book, put yourself out there and go sell!

CHAPTER SIX

Business Is Business

Business is business. What does that mean? In literal terms, it means that all business is the same regardless of what field or industry you are in or what product or service you sell. In more practical terms, it means that life isn't fair, only the tough survive, and you had better be looking out for your best interests because nobody else will. The law of business is the law of the jungle: it's survival of the fittest, and only the strong survive.

As the captain of your ship, your only responsibility is to you, your ship, your crew, and your cargo; and making sure that your ship safely reaches its destination. Nothing more and nothing less. Nothing more means you aren't responsible for any other ships at sea, and you certainly aren't responsible for their cargo. If you can assist other ships along your journey, do so, but do so cautiously and only if it doesn't interrupt your itinerary or put your journey, your crew, your cargo, or your destination in jeopardy. Nothing less means you are 100 percent responsible for your ship and the safety of your cargo; don't allow any distractions to set you off course.

I have bought and sold a dozen businesses, I've purchased and sold over a hundred million dollars in real estate, and have owned a multitude of businesses in various industries. Those experiences have convinced me that all businesses are relatively the same. Regardless of what product or service you are selling, the same basic business principles apply. You have a product or a service that you are selling; you have to market and sell that product or service; and then you have to service whatever you have sold, and try to make a profit in the process. It's a pretty simple concept. What this should tell you is that it is much more important to know more about business than it is to know about the product or service you are selling. Don't get me wrong, it is far better to know as much about both as you possibly can, but if you don't have a good grasp and knowledge of business, you will most certainly fail.

I have been involved all of my life in construction, real estate, and development. I have also spent about fifteen years of my life in the restaurant and hospitality business, as well as retail and marinas. My hobby has always been agriculture. I have a pretty broad range of experience in many different businesses, and I can tell you firsthand that each and every one of those businesses had exactly the very same business principles and fundamentals.

I've always done extremely well in construction and real estate, but my first year in the restaurant business I lost over $300,000! If that rate of loss had continued, I would have been sunk in no time. I had never been in the restaurant business before in my life, but like most people, I always thought that it would be a cool business to be in. I thought I could hire some good people with extensive restaurant experience, and turn the management over to them; what could be so hard? That was my second mistake. If you are wondering what my first mistake was, it was getting into the restaurant business in the first place. I was already all in, and having never failed at business before, I quickly realized that I was going to have to get very serious about what I was doing. I realized that although I did have a pretty good management team, including a really great chef, what I didn't understand at the time was that regardless of how much restaurant experience anyone has or how great a chef that someone is, it doesn't mean that he or she has a clue about business, and they often don't.

I didn't know anything about running a restaurant; in fact, other than a dishwashing job when I was twelve years old and a fast food gig when I was a teenager, I had never worked in a restaurant before. Interestingly enough, in that first job as a dishwasher earning $1.65 per hour, the guy I was working for was named Ronald Reagan. I recall that when he hired me he introduced himself: "I'm Ronald Reagan—you know, like the actor." I had no idea who Ronald Reagan the actor was, but I sure did a few years later when he was elected president of the United States; that's probably where my conservative politics first began.

I may not have known anything about running a restaurant, but I did know a lot about business; business is my forte. I quickly realized that my expertise in running a construction company was exactly the same knowledge and expertise that I needed to run a restaurant. (I would add that a really good chef is a big help as well). After that first year, I did some serious soul searching, took the business very seriously, sunk another million dollars into improvements and control systems, and by the end of the second year, we broke even; by the third year I had made everything back that I had previously lost. The restaurant went on to be a huge success every year after that.

I would say however, that I've been asked a thousand times, "Whatever made you want to get into the restaurant business?" My classic response has always been, "Stupidity." I have owned several restaurants, and I can tell you that it's easier to make a good living pounding nails.

Whether you own or manage a business or are simply managing your family or just your own life, you will find yourself dealing with people on some business level on a daily basis. Even if you are only a student going to school or college, you are still dealing with other students, teachers, and faculty. You are in daily negotiations whether you realize it or not. Negotiating with your parents to use their car or to help pay your college tuition is still negotiation. Negotiating with your teachers to secure a better grade is still negotiation. Any exchange of commerce can be a negotiation, getting a job or a promotion is a negotiation.

Master the art of negotiation. Understand what it is you really want, and figure out what your opponent (the person you are negotiating with) really wants, then find the common ground. Never cry over what's fair and what's not fair; business is business, and it's usually not fair. It's up to you to negotiate the best deal for yourself or your business. You can rest assured that your opponent (the person you are negotiating against) is going to try and negotiate what's best for him- or herself, and that usually isn't what's best for you. You will always have your hands more than full just taking care of yourself and your business, let alone spending any time worrying about your opponent's business. I realize that may sound a little harsh, but life is tough and business isn't for the faint of heart.

One word of advice when you are trying to negotiate a deal, or get what you want; when you get the answer you want; accept it, then shut up, or hang up! Another word of advice when dealing with your competitor or your adversary; when they are screwing up, or making mistakes; shut up and get out of their way!

How many times have you heard people complain about the job they have? It's not fair, I work harder than everyone else, and I'm not being fairly compensated for what I do. That is the great thing about America being a democracy; you don't have to stay in any job you don't like if you are able to secure a better one. A job is a negotiation and an agreement between employer and employee. The employee agrees to provide a service to the employer, and the employer agrees to pro-vide a job for a specific compensation. If the employee doesn't like the agreement, he or she can either try to renegotiate the compensation or employment arrangement or can they can quit.

I had a carpenter who was working for me back in the mid-1990s, and at the time he was making about $19.00 per hour, which was a pretty competitive carpenter's wage at that time. In addition to his hourly wage, I paid for half of his health and dental insurance, contributed to his 401K retirement, and he also received a week's paid vacation and paid holidays. If he had been with me for over two years, his vacation time would have increased to two weeks each year, and he would have likely been eligible for a raise. It was a pretty decent trade job by any standards at the time.

This carpenter's name was Mike, and Mike had been with me for about a year, was a pretty decent carpenter, and was by all appearances a fairly good employee. One day Mike came into my office and gave me a two-week notice that he was going to quit. I told Mike that I appreciated the notice, and asked him why he was quitting and what his plans were. I must say that his response was a new one for me, and took me completely off guard: no, he didn't have a better job lined up, and he wasn't leaving because he thought he was being underpaid for his work. He was quitting because he thought that he was making me too much money. He went on to explain that he knew what I charged for our work; he said it was obvious that I was making a very good living, and for whatever reason all of this didn't sit well with him. I really couldn't believe what I was hearing; I wished Mike well and told him that he should be working for an unsuccessful company. An odd look came across Mike's face, and he asked what I was talking about. I told him that it seemed to me from his comments that he would feel better about himself if he was working for a fly-by-night contractor who was driving an old beat up pickup truck and living in a trailer, a contractor who didn't pay any employee benefits, didn't have any steady work for him, and bounced his payroll checks. That didn't sit too well with Mike, and he wanted to debate the issue with me. I again wished him well and told him that I wasn't sure how we were going to get along without him, but from that day forward we were going to have to try.

Mike obviously had a chip on his shoulder. One thing I haven't mentioned is that, like many other tradesmen that have worked for me over the years, Mike had previously tried to be in business for himself as a contractor and failed. When Mike was in business for himself he bid his jobs trying to make a good wage, not understanding everything else that needed to be considered in his estimates in order to build a successful business. Mike thought that he should add up what his materials cost, add his hourly labor costs, and ad any subcontractor costs; he may have even added another 10 percent to his bid thinking that was his profit. What Mike didn't realize was that his estimates should have been about 50 percent greater to cover all of his indirect costs and then make a reasonable profit. Mike didn't understand that even though his wage was $19 per hour, his actual cost to me was about $28.50 per hour, once I added in his burden (work comp & general liability insurance, FICA, and employee benefits, etc…). As I previously noted, Mike was a good carpenter but a terrible businessman. To Mike, the success of my business only highlighted his failed attempts at running his own contracting business. Running a business isn't for everyone; someone can know everything about his or her trade and still not have a clue as to what it takes to be in business.

He who takes all the risk deserves all of the reward: that is such a true statement. However, most anyone who's never been that person taking all the risk never seems to find the justice in that statement. The person who starts the company, risks everything, puts up his or her life savings, and has to sign on the bottom line deserves to reap the rewards if and when the business comes to fruition. God only knows that if for any reason things don't go well that person is the one left holding the bag and has everything to lose. Having success and losing it is much worse than never having it at all.

If you are in business for yourself; expect your competition to try and crush you into nonexistence; it is in their interest for self-preservation. If the opportunity arises, don't hesitate to crush your competition if it's in your interest to do so. Believe me, if you fail at something or your business fails, your competition may smile to your face and say they are sorry for what you are going through, but you can bet your bottom dollar that most of them are high-fiving behind your back.

That said, if you can help your competition without jeopardizing your own self-interests or your own business, do so—but do so cautiously. You can learn a lot from your competition, and you can get a great deal out of building alliances.

Several years ago I went to an auction of equipment from one of my competitors who had gone out of business. The competitor was a guy who had started his construction business about the same time that I started mine and, all things considered, we were fairly friendly competitors—but still competitors. The way I saw it at the time was that his going out of business left a bigger piece of the pie for my company. I was pretty excited about going to the auction; I had secured a letter of credit from my bank, and had planned on purchasing at least a hundred thousand dollars' worth of his equipment. But I remember distinctly how I felt when I pulled into the parking lot at the auction house; I started getting this really sick feeling in my stomach. I started realizing that this could have just as easily been me and my company losing everything.

This competitor was a guy about the same age as me, with a similar story; a young guy with a nice family whose business skyrocketed in a very short period of time. Unfortunately he didn't deal with overnight success very well and ended up going down a dark path, getting messed up with drugs and some bad people. One thing led to another, and before he knew it he'd lost everything.

I vividly remember walking into the auction warehouse; it was a bitter cold spring morning, the cold concrete floors sent a chill through my body. As I looked around, I could have used everything they were auctioning, but I couldn't get the sick feeling out of my gut. How does this happen? I kept asking myself. It shook the hell out of me, and I couldn't bring myself to purchase anything. As I left there empty-handed, I knew that the trip was not a waste of my time; I had learned a valuable lesson. From then on I refocused my energy on my business and vowed to do everything to prevent that from ever happening to me.

Never forget that the expression "business is business" also means that when you own a company and are extending credit to another company, you are extending credit to *that business* and very likely not the business owner (unless you have had him or her sign a personal guarantee). Business is a calculated risk, and if you are a smart professional it's incumbent on you to protect yourself. If you are doing business with another company and they manage to stay alive, you will most likely always be paid; but if that company fails, you will likely not get paid; it's the risk that both businesses take. Half of the small businesses in this country fail every day. And when they do, it's a domino effect of vendors that don't get paid. Your first reaction is likely to get mad at the guy whose business failed and who wasn't able to pay you. What's the point in that? That guy likely has many more problems he's dealing with; whatever sum you lost out on is not his top priority. You have some responsibility because you extended him credit and may not have adequately secured the credit you extended to his company. Don't forget that his business owing you money doesn't necessarily mean that the guy who owns the company owes you money. I doubt very seriously that he ever planned it that way, and if you weren't a smart enough of businessperson to protect yourself from any potentially failing businesses that you would be likely to deal with, you have no one to blame but yourself. If I had a dollar for every thousand dollars I have had to write off over the years, from customers who went bankrupt or out of business and couldn't pay, I'd have a much healthier bank account. There is almost never any recourse, and litigation is timely, expensive, and usually offers no satisfaction. Some people take it personally; It's almost never personal and it shouldn't be taken personally; when a business fails and is unable to meet all of its financial obligations, it's often part of a chain reaction that started with creditors that owed that business money, and failed to meet their obligations.

Being an entrepreneur and being in business is always a risk, and with any risk there is always a potential of failure. If it weren't for people willing to take risks, we would likely still be stuck in the stone ages. You may be surprised by some people in history who had failed businesses, or filed for bankruptcy, and then later went on to be hugely successful. These individuals obviously learned from their mistakes and seldom made the same mistakes twice. They not only learned but also didn't give up; they picked themselves back up, dusted themselves off, and got back in the saddle.

Honest Abe Lincoln may have been a great president, but he was not a good businessman. In 1832, Lincoln tried his hat at being a shop owner. Lincoln and his partner bought up the inventory of other stores on credit, but their sales ended up being dismal, resulting in his creditors taking him to court. Lincoln lost his only two remaining assets, a horse and some surveying gear. Lincoln is not alone as a politician in his financial shortcomings; Ulysses S. Grant went bankrupt after leaving office when his investment banking partner swindled him. And Thomas Jefferson filed for bankruptcy several times, including after leaving office, likely from throwing around a lot of cash on food and wine. William McKinley went on to win the White House only three years after filing for bankruptcy.

Automobile legend Henry Ford's automobile enterprise filed for bankruptcy in 1901. Ford wasn't the only automobile magnate who experienced bankruptcy; William Crapo Durant, founder of General Motors, took a massive hit during the Great Depression, which saw his fortune drop from $120 million to bankruptcy! H. J. Heinz filed for bankruptcy in 1875, and then he and his brother started making ketchup, and today the H. J. Heinz Company takes in over $10 billion in annual revenue. Walt Disney first began his film studio business in Kansas City, Missouri, back in 1922, making short advertising films and cartoons under the name Laugh-O-Gram Studio. Disney couldn't cover his overhead and went bankrupt the following year. It's no secret what Walt Disney went on to accomplish.

No doubt all of these entrepreneurs hit some significant roadblocks along the way, but they overcame those roadblocks and went on to accomplish great success by anyone's standards.

Why do so many businesses fail? After being in business myself for over twenty-five years, it seems elementary; there is a formula for failure and a formula for success. This book should give you a good road map for the formula for success; so let me share with you the formula for failure; the ten top reasons that businesses fail:

1. Lack of experience or knowledge. Many people start their businesses with the misconception that they know all they need to know about how to start a business. They fail to comprehend that it takes a strong knowledge and understanding not only about the business they are going into but also about business itself and accounting.

2. Undercapitalization. Starting any business takes capital, and some businesses take a lot of capital. It's not just the amount of money it takes to open your business, get all your legal ducks in order, and so on. It's also important to have a cash reserve to cover operational costs for the first year, plus enough reserves for the proprietor to live off for however long it takes the company to generate a positive cash flow; this is often longer than a year. People often have a misconception about what they can and can't borrow from lenders in order to capitalize their businesses, and often grossly underestimate the necessary capital that will be required of them.

3. Poor management. I don't care what anyone says about the experience he or she might have in running a business; if you have never had to meet a payroll yourself you are an inexperienced beginner. If you own the company, you are the CEO, and you will find yourself dealing with issues you may have never contemplated—everything from financing to purchasing, sales, production, marketing and advertising, staffing, legal issues, and a plethora of human resource management issues.

4. Poor planning. Every business must have a strategic plan; that plan should begin with a very realistic budget. The plan must be based on facts and current information, and a well-thought-out educated projection. All too often business owners try to "wing it," and that seldom works.

5. Poor location. Location, location, location! Not all businesses require a certain location, but for those that do the bad location can be the kiss of death. Two businesses that absolutely must have the right location are restaurants and retail establishments. People often choose the cheaper location because of being undercapitalized; this is a mistake you cannot afford to make. You are better off leasing a building for $10,000 per month in the right location than one for $2,000 a month in a mediocre location. Think about it: most all of your other expenses are relatively the same, but the right location can make all the difference in your gross sales and easily make up the increased cost of the space you might be leasing or purchasing.

6. Poor marketing and advertising. Every business must get its message out to potential customers; how else will they know about you? First you need to know who your customers are, and then determine the best way to reach those customers. If your target market is baby boomers, you would use advertising to specifically target baby boomers. However, if your target market is teenagers or young adults, you would probably use an entirely different avenue of marketing. Advertising is a must, but it is also a very costly and very risky expense; once you've spent a dollar on advertising it is usually gone; and if you don't get any results from it, it was a big waste of money. Many businesses forget to invest any marketing in their past and existing customers; that is a big mistake. Internet advertising and a good website is a must in today's market.

7. Unrealistic expectations. Business owners often have a habit of being overly optimistic, which results in unrealistic expectations, which can lead to big problems. This is why a very realistic budget and projection is imperative. Unrealistic expectations will only set you up for failure.

8. Failure to adapt to a changing market. Potential customers are fickle people; their wants and needs can change overnight. Technology often changes in an instant. No company should ever find itself in the position of being the last company in the world selling buggy whips. Companies that have been in business for a considerable length of time can often get complacent, disassociated from what their customers are really looking for; that can be the kiss of death.

9. Growing too quickly. Some companies' growth is faster than they are ready for, or they try to expand before they are ready or capable. Some business owners often confuse success with their realistic ability to expand their businesses. Slow and steady growth is always the best course; don't get overextended.

10. Inability to control costs. This is where a good business plan and a realistic budget and projections can come into place. Growing businesses often find that their costs and expenses get out of control—and often before the business owner realizes it.

Accurate profit and loss statements each and every month are a must, and can be a good tool to help keep costs in line; at the very least, if costs are getting out of control, a good review of accurate profits and losses will assist a business owner in recognizing increased or out-of-control costs. These monthly P&L statements should be completed within ten days at the end of each month or sooner, depending on the business and industry you are in. Businesses who wait until the end of the year to compile a financial statement, will often find that by then it's too late to make any meaningful difference.

Don't cry over spilled milk. You can't change the past; you can only improve the future and avoid making the same mistakes twice. Don't sweat the things in life that you have no control over or that you can't change. That is a lesson that didn't come easy for Roy Raymond. Raymond was a graduate student from the Stanford School of Business in California who felt rather embarrassed when it came to purchasing beautiful lingerie from any department store for his wife. So in 1977 Raymond decided to create a store that made a man feel comfortable when purchasing women's lingerie. With a $40,000 bank loan, and another $40,000 he borrowed from relatives, Roy Raymond opened the first Victoria's Secret store. The décor was Victorian, designed with wood paneled walls; it had a friendly staff. Instead of bras and panties being hung on a sterile rack, they were paired together in all sizes and mounted on frames or displayed on manikins. Attention to detail was meticulous, and the stores were very inviting to men and women alike.

The first Victoria's Secret opened at the Stanford Shopping Center near San Francisco; soon three other stores opened. By the end of the first year in business, the company had earned $500,000. In 1984, after five years in business, the company had six stores, a forty-two-page catalog, and was grossing $6 million per year. Raymond sold the company for a measly $4 million to Leslie Wexner, creator of the Limited chain of clothing stores. Ten years later Victoria's Secret had become the largest American lingerie retailer, topping $1 billion in annual sales. In 2009 Victoria's Secret was worth over $5 billion.

In 1984, Roy Raymond started a new business endeavor called My Child's Destiny, a retail store for children. That business went bankrupt in 1986. On August 26th, 1993, Roy Raymond leaped to his death, by jumping off the Golden Gate Bridge at the age of forty-six.

Life isn't fair, and business certainly isn't fair. If you are going to succeed in life, and in business, you had better accept the fact that life isn't fair and get over it. Life is whatever you make of it, and if you make bad decisions, you had better be prepared for the consequences. In the case of Roy Raymond my question is, why would you ever sell a business that is making you $500,000 a year for a measly $4 million? I'm sure he had his reasons; $4 million surely sounded like a lot of money. But in retrospect it wasn't that much.

Business is unforgiving; you either make it or you don't. If you are successful, it's only going to be because you make it happen. You make more right decisions than wrong, offer a good product or service at a competitive price in a favorable market. A little luck never hurts, and timing is everything!

I learned an extremely valuable lesson about timing—or, I should say, an extremely expensive lesson about timing. In 2006, I began developing a luxury condominium hotel complex adjacent to my restaurant and entertainment complex on Lake of the Ozarks in Missouri. The project was collectively about a $60 million development and included a five-star hotel, a yacht club/marina, a spa, a swimming pool, fitness and recreation areas, a convention center, an outdoor amphitheater, a movie theater, restaurants, and retail shops. It was by far the nicest and most aggressive project that had ever been built in the Lake of the Ozarks resort market. My restaurant and entertainment complex had already experienced over a decade of prosperity, and this new development was only a natural extension of that.

I had been buying up properties for several years—mainly waterfront homes and businesses, ultimately including over twenty-five properties. All of these properties were razed (torn down) to make way for my new development, one of the primary elements of which was an all-suite, condominium hotel. The plan was to sell luxury hotel suites to vacationers for use when they visited the lake and, when they weren't using them they had the option for us to rent them out and we would split the revenues with them. We were going to build this luxury complex and sell off the units to help zero out the debt, then maintain the management operation of the hotel, and my surrounding businesses. This would also provide very nice lodging directly adjacent to our entertainment complex, thereby increasing our year-round business by hosting business conferences, conventions, and other events.

It was a great plan; after all, my restaurant entertainment complex had grown to be extremely successful, with plenty of cash flow. I worked out the financing details with my bank, and as part of our business plan, we would presell $15 million worth of our condotel suites to ensure the viability of the project. By the middle of 2007, we had successfully sold $15 million in units, which included forty-seven units at an average price of $320,000 per unit. All sales were hard contracts, with a 10 percent nonrefundable deposit.

My business plan was that we would close on all of the pre-sold units and use those proceeds to pay down the debt. I would then have the ability to draw back, up to about half of those funds as needed to cover our initial debt service, operational start-up costs, and a substantial marketing campaign during our stabilization period.

It was a great idea, a great project, a great plan: $15 million in presales at an average price of $320,000 for a 750-square-foot suite, with hard contracts and real deposits, and adjacent to a business that had been very successful for over ten years! It sounded like a no-brainer to me.

But then there is timing; and as I have previously noted, timing is everything. We finished the hotel in the third quarter of 2008. And anyone who was over the age of ten at that time knows that the world as we knew it came to an end in the third quarter of 2008. I wouldn't say that my world came to an end, but I was hanging on by a thread. Surprisingly enough, we did have twenty-five buyers honor their contracts and close on their units as agreed. However, twenty-two of my buyers breached their contracts and were either unwilling or unable to close on their units due to the global economic collapse.

This immediately left a $7 million hole in my business plan. To make matters worse, the government quickly imposed much tighter restrictions on lenders, which completely tied my lenders' hands on providing any more capital for the project. To add insult to injury, tourism across the country came to a standstill, people cut back on vacations and summer trips to the lake, and businesses definitely cut back on conferences and conventions. I found myself at a major crossroads in my life, and with a dilemma that I wasn't quite sure I would survive. The year 2009 was supposed to be one of "hope and change," the government was sinking a trillion dollars into what it referred to as stimulus package, and touted that the summer of 2009 was going to be the "summer of recovery." Being the optimistic entrepreneur that I am, I sunk another million dollars into my business in hopes that we would quickly get through the Great Recession in short order and that the stimulus would jump-start the economy as promised. As we all now know, no promise the government ever made has turned out to be so misguided.

Ten words you never want to hear: "I am from the government, and I'm here to help." No thanks.

By the third quarter of 2009, it was painfully obvious to me that the economy wasn't going to recover any time soon. I had a $400,000 interest payment coming due, and not enough cash reserves to pay much more than that, and we were headed into the very slow winter months. This is when I found myself eye to eye with the eye of the hurricane!

For the next couple of months there wasn't a week that passed that I wasn't in my bank's conference room or board room, reminding the bank executives that they were my partners in this venture, that we were all married to it rather we liked it or not. I certainly hadn't caused the global economic meltdown and I certainly wasn't in a position to fix it on my own.

As if things couldn't be any worse; my construction company was a co-guarantor on the loan for the resort, which created a potential problem as I was in the process of finishing up a multi-million dollar custom home for a very good client. This project started out as a luxury spec house, which meant that my company owned the property and had taken out the construction loan, with the intent of selling the house upon completion. However in the early stages of construction, one of my previous clients decided that they wanted to purchase the house and make some substantial changes to custom tailor the house to suit them. These changes more than doubled the cost and size of the project, so our clients paid considerable deposits for much of the increased cost of these changes, however our contract required that my company would maintain ownership of the property while it was under construction, and keep the existing construction loan in place until the project was completed; at which time the new owners would then get their funding in place and close on the house. This was a good thing; everything was moving along ok, and we were getting close to completing the project. Then the economy collapsed and I found myself in hard ball negotiations with my lenders on my resort, and I didn't know what the outcome of those negotiations would be. Since my company still owned the house, this could have created serious unintended consequences to my client's interest in the house if I wasn't able to negotiate an amicable resolution with my bank, and was forced into bankruptcy. To make matters worse, the design and finishes of this house changed and grew week by week, which caused delays, and created substantial cost overruns. My only recourse was to meet with my customers, explain the situation to them, apologize for the predicament this put them in, and advise them that it was in their best interest if they could close on the house as soon as possible, before it was finished. This would protect their interest in the house, while we worked diligently to complete the project. My clients were understandably not happy about this situation, but agreed that it was the only responsible way to proceed. We did finish the house for them a few months later, but I knew that I had let them down, and that I very much regret.

After months of bare-knuckle negotiations with the lenders who financed my resort development, we finally came to an amicable resolution; I relinquished nearly $25 million of my own equity in the development, and over half a million dollars in deposits I had in accounts with the bank at the time. In turn, I was released from any further liability or any potential deficiency. I also agreed to act as a consultant for the first six months to ensure a smooth transition. The first week of January 2010 I relinquished ownership of the resort development that I had spent twelve years of my life bringing to fruition, and had invested twelve years of blood, sweat, tears, and treasure in. It was definitely one of the darkest, and hardest times of my life.

Like I've said, life isn't fair, and business certainly isn't fair; it throws you some curve balls in the blink of an eye, and you either face them head on, adapt and overcome, or you go down hard. I did what I had to do, which by any savvy businessperson's perspective was working a miracle. As traumatic as it was, it could have certainly been much worse. It could have easily forced me into bankruptcy, and I could have lost everything I've ever worked for. As it turned out, I was able to keep my good credit intact; and I was able to keep whatever assets that weren't cross collateralized by that loan. It left me the ability to pick up and rebuild my life. The months and years that followed were challenging to say the least, but I took them one day and one challenge at a time, and overcame.

I could have, and would have been justified to sue all of the twenty-two buyers who breached their contracts. But for their breach, I would have been in good shape; the extra $7 million I was owed at the time would have made a world of difference, and surely would have enabled me to overcome the downturn in the economy. But I also understand that business is business, and you can't get blood out of a turnip; a judgment is only good if you can collect it, and the lawsuits would have likely been costly and drawn out for an extended period of time; and time was not my friend. I doubt any of the buyers under contract intended to breach their contracts, or cause me these damages when they made the agreements; but the Great Recession changed life as we knew it for everyone. Everything rolled downhill in a chain reaction; twenty-two people owed me collectively over $7 million dollars, and due to circumstances that were likely beyond their control, they breached their agreements with me, and for whatever reason they were unable to pay me what I was owed. This all created a terrible chain reaction which adversely impacted my businesses, and ultimately resulted in me losing most of my life's work. I took whatever steps I could to protect my future; I worked out whatever I could with my vendors, and negotiated an amicable settlement with my lenders'; and that was that. What can I say? Business is business, it isn't fair, and it isn't for the weak at heart.

It was an expensive but very valuable lesson. In hindsight I'm not sure what I could have or would have done differently. No point in crying over spilled milk, tomorrow is another day.

❯Action Steps

1. Review any contracts or lease agreements you are currently legally bound to, and what the penalties will be if you breach the agreement. Go over them with an attorney if necessary.

2. Identify 3 things in your personal life; that you have failed at or wish you had done much differently, and identify what it is that you would have done differently in hindsight.

3. Identify 3 things in your professional career, or business that you have failed at or wish you had done much differently, and identify what it is that you would have done differently in hindsight.

4. Identify something important that you dwell on, or something that your friends and family believe you dwell on; then identify why you dwell on it, and what you can do to change that.

Reccognizing your weaknesses, and acknowledging your failures is the first step in making lasting improvements. If you don't think you've had any failures in life or in business, you either haven't ever put yourself out there, or you aren't thinking hard enough.

Understand that as the CEO of any business you have but one obligation, and that is to your stockholders, even if the only stockholder is yourself. Business is tough, and if you are going to be in the arena, you had better be tough or toughen up. Being in business is about making a profit; business isn't always fair, and it shouldn't be taken personally.

Write down your responses to Action Steps 2, 3 & 4; then make a note to review the agreements listed in Action Step 1, and make every effort to do so once you have finished this book.

CHAPTER SEVEN

Know Your Numbers

Know your numbers; know everything about them. I don't mean just addition, subtraction, multiplication, and division, though those you need to know backward and forward. It's also imperative to have a clear understanding of percentages, markups, and margins. If you don't know them, learn them; reach out to a teacher, an accountant, or a business coach and have them explain them to you as many times as necessary until you are confident that you have a real grasp on them.

As the captain of your ship, if you don't know your numbers, you won't be able to properly calculate your trip or chart your course, and you will surely get lost at sea.

Math is one of the few things in life that is exact, and the numbers never lie. You can't get by in life without having an understanding of numbers, and if you are in business for yourself you must master them.

When I first began my construction business in the back of my garage, back in 1989, I thought I had a pretty good understanding of math—certainly, I thought, enough to get by. I knew that accounting wasn't my strong point, but thought I could hire an accountant to handle that boring stuff for me. My first year in business I thought I was doing pretty well; I put myself on a $36,000 salary and it seemed that my business was doing OK as well. At the end of the first year, I hired an accountant to figure out if I was making any money.

This was back before many businesses were using computers, and having grown up in the pre-tech era, I certainly didn't know much about using them, so my record keeping was basically a checkbook and a box of receipts. I communicated back and forth with my accountant for a couple of weeks, and he was able to compile my first year-end profit and loss statement and balance sheet as well as my year-end tax return. We got together to go over everything, and he had compiled everything for me in a nice and neat format; to my surprise, I was very happy to see that not only had I paid myself a $36,000 salary but also the business had made $87,000. My reaction was, Wow, I actually made $123,000 in my very first year of business!

I was confused, however, because I didn't have an extra $87,000 in the bank; in fact, I was lucky if I had $10,000. Where did the rest of the money go? I asked. My accountant patiently explained, step by step, that as I was growing my business I was investing in my business. Most of the money the company earned was used for buying new tools and equipment that was needed, and I had some outstanding receivables that I hadn't yet collected. I started to digest that reality—that as I made money I was spending it on assets needed to grow my business rather than what I had thought, which was that the money I was spending on equipment was simply a business expense.

Once I got past that lesson in Accounting 101, I was still feeling pretty good about having made over $100,000 in my first year in business. Then my accountant hit me between the eyes with the bad news! It seemed that even after my expenses, and depreciation from all of the equipment I had purchased that year; I owed the IRS about $30,000!

I just about had a heart attack! I didn't have an extra $30,000 laying around. I only had my $10,000 reserve, which put me in one hell of a bad spot.

As tough a spot as that put me in I was able to earn my way through it by working harder and smarter, and in the long run was thankful for the valuable lesson I had learned. I realize that I had a lot more to learn about accounting and taxes, and that it wasn't nearly good enough for me to simply have a good accountant to figure things out at the end of each year; I had to become an accountant myself. My accountant became one of my very best friends and is still my accountant today.

I immediately realized that I had to completely revamp the way I had been doing business in the past if I was going to grow my business into the business I knew it could be. I hired a full-time bookkeeper and computerized not only my accounting system but my estimating and job costing. I also made a conscious decision to hang my tool belt up and focus all of my attention on managing and growing my business.

Accounting was never something that I thought I would have much use for, the thought of crunching numbers all day bored the hell out of me. I once asked my accountant friend, "What on earth made you want to become an accountant?" He replied that he too disliked accounting, and would much prefer being a pro golfer. He then commented that as much as he disliked accounting, he loved business, and you can't succeed at business without accounting. He then disclosed that he only became an accountant to learn about the many different businesses there are and to create an opportunity for himself to get involved in these many different businesses—and, when the opportunity presented itself, to own some of those businesses. Today he owns an interest in several businesses. I have always taken those comments to heart, and ever since have taken a real interest in accounting; I have made every effort to develop a real understanding of it and how it relates to my businesses.

My accountant also taught me a valuable lesson, one that I refer to throughout this book: business and careers are simply a tool to help us get what we want out of life. My accountant's passion in life is playing golf. His accounting business affords him lots of time and opportunity to pursue his passion, to play a lot of golf.

My next accounting lesson was to understand how a profit and loss statement works. Once you understand it, it's not too difficult. Gross sales (excluding sales taxes) less the cost of goods sold, equals gross profit; gross profit less expenses equals' net profit.

Profit & Loss Statement

Revenue

Sales	$1,000,000
Cost of Goods Sold (example: 55%)	$550,000
Gross Profit	**$450,000**

Expenses

Payroll	$100,000
Payroll Burden	$20,000
Legal & Accounting & Fee's	$10,000
Utilities	$15,000
Marketing & Advertising	$55,000
Interest expense	$15,000
Rent	$120,000
Insurance	$45,000
Total Expenses	**$380,000**
Operating Income	**$70,000 (7%)**
Other Expenses (misc.)	$5,000
Depreciation (loss in value of assets)	$5,000
Net Income	**$60,000 (6%)**

A profit and loss statement seems simple enough, and it is, so long as you understand what goes where. Below is a very brief explanation of most everything that goes into such a statement.

Sales. Sales are pretty self-explanatory; they are the total revenue earned in a given time for the product or service you sell. This number would not include anything like loans or owner contributions. It would include revenues earned and invoiced but possibly not yet received. Depending on the business you are in, it would also include any work in progress for money you are owed but have not yet billed. It would usually not include sales tax collected (and if it did, then the offsetting sales tax expense would need to be included under expenses).

Cost of Goods Sold. This is your direct cost associated with the product you are selling. This is the true and actual cost of the product you are selling before you mark it up and sell it. (Example: If you sell widgets for ten dollars, and you buy them or make them at a cost of five dollars, the five dollars is your cost of goods sold. If you had sold 100,000 widgets, your sales would be $1 million, and your cost of goods sold would be $500,000). These are your direct costs, and do not include your indirect costs or other unrelated operating or business expenses. Payroll usually is not a part of your cost of goods sold, depending on the business or industry you are in, unless that payroll is directly related to the product or service that you are selling. It may include payroll to service, manufacture or install a product, but it would not include any administrative or related payroll.

Expenses. Your expenses are the indirect costs associated with your ongoing business operations and sales of your product or service. This comprises all costs you incur other than the cost of the product or service you are selling (that is, everything other than the cost of the widget). This would include everything from payroll, to insurance, advertising, rent, fees, utilities, and so on. Expenses would include any administrative, management, sales, and clerical payroll, but it would usually not include any payroll directly related to the product or service you are selling (manufacturing or trade labor).

Burden. Payroll burden refers to the cost incurred for your payroll, that are in addition to your actual hourly or salaried payroll costs; this includes employer tax contributions (FICA), workers' compensation insurance, general liability insurance, unemployment insurance, health and dental insurance, uniforms, and employee benefits—including paid holidays, vacation, retirement contribution, and any other paid days off that an employee receives. It may also include any vehicle allowance and any other costs associated directly with each employee. (Example: An employee who earns twenty dollars per hour will likely cost his employer $thirty dollars per hour, or about 50 percent more than what the employee actually receives); so in this case the burden cost would be 50% greater than the actual payroll cost.

Cash & Acrual Accounting. Cash accounting includes all cash paid and received. Acrual accounting includes all cash paid and received, plus all cash you are due (receivables) and all cash you owe (payables).

Balance Sheet. The balance sheet is a compilation of all of your assets and liabilities at a given time. This would include the total value of all assets, including cash, furniture, fixtures, equipment, stocks, notes receivable, deposits, work in progress (that is, is the amount of costs incurred on something that will ultimately be billed out but has not yet been), capital improvements, and owners' contributions, less all debt, accounts payables, and depreciation. Here are some sample categories and simple definitions for a balance sheet:

Balance Sheet

Assets. Basically, all of your stuff.

Current assets. Cash, receivables, or work in progress that will become cash within one year.

Fixed assets. Assets used to make cash; furniture, fixtures, and equipment (less accumulated depreciation).

Accumulated depreciation. The amount your stuff has depreciated in value over the time since you purchased it. Real estate ground (land) does not depreciate; real estate buildings and improvements usually depreciate at 1/40 per year; and furniture, fixtures, and equipment depreciate based on their realistic lifespan—usually not more than 1/7 each year.

Other assets. Inventory, deposits, etc.

Total Assets. The combination of your liabilities and equity.

Liabilities. Basically, whatever you owe on all of your stuff that is due within a given year.

Current liabilities. Cash to be used within one year, payables, current portion of long-term debt.

Long-term Liabilities. Loan balances on assets that will not be paid off within a given year.

Equity. The value of your stuff, less depreciation, less what you still owe on it.

Stock. The value of your company's stock; typically what you valued your stock at when you established the business.

Retained earnings. Money previously earned that hasn't been paid out.

Stockholder contributions. Money you have contributed to your company, other than your initial stock.

Net Income. Amount of money you have earned in a given year.

Total Liabilities and Equity. The value of the equity in the stuff you own plus the debt you owe on your stuff; the gross value of your stuff.

Net Worth. The net value of all of your stuff; what would all of your stuff be worth if you sold it today (not what you paid for it, but what could you sell it for today; that is the depreciated value of your stuff), after you pay off any debt you owe on your stuff. The original cost/value of all your assets, less depreciation, and less the debt you still owe on all of your stuff; equals your Net Worth.

Depreciation is the loss of value in an asset that occurs over time. When you purchase an asset you set it up on a depreciation schedule, and depreciate it over the life expectancy of the asset. (Example: You pay $1,000 for a copy machine, and the life expectancy of the copy machine is five years; you would then divide the $1,000 by 5, and depreciate that amount each year until it has depreciated to a zero value; $1,000 divided by 5 equals $200; as such you would depreciate $200 each year for the copier). Typically furniture, fixtures, and equipment depreciate over seven years, and real estate (excluding land) depreciates over forty years. Land does not depreciate at all.

You will recall that earlier in this chapter I talked about the end of the first year I was in business. My profit and loss statement indicated that I made $87,000, but I only had $10,000 in cash reserves, and couldn't understand how I made such a large amount of money, but didn't have anything to show for it. A cash flow analysis will help explain where your cash is, and where it went. A cash flow analysis is basically what you have spent your money on, or where it is currently; this is a bit more complicated, but extremely important. There are a great number of things that impact your cash flow both positively and negatively.

Cash Flow Analysis

Operating cash flow. Net Income is a positive, but there are adjustments to reconcile net income to cash.

Depreciation is a cash flow positive because it is an expense that wasn't actually paid for out of your cash reserves.

Increase in accounts receivable is a cash flow negative because you are financing what people owe you, so all you have is a note (invoice) due to you that has not yet been converted to cash.

Increase in accounts payable is a cash flow positive because your suppliers are financing you; in other words, you haven't yet spent your cash to pay your suppliers.

Decrease in inventory is a cash flow positive because you have used inventory you had on hand, thereby selling your inventory and avoiding spending cash to purchase inventory that would have otherwise been required.

Increase in inventory is a cash flow negative because you have now used cash to purchase inventory.

Investing. Capital expenditures including any real property (your stuff: real estate, furniture, fixtures, and equipment); it greatly affects your cash flow because you are using your cash to purchase assets (your stuff).

A vehicle purchase is a cash flow negative because you are potentially using cash to purchase an asset.

Trading in a vehicle for a new vehicle is a cash flow positive because you are getting cash value for a trade (assuming you have completely depreciated, and paid off the trade-in).

Capital improvements to property are a cash flow negative because you are spending your cash on improving your assets.

Financing. Financing capital expenditures will also affect your cash flow because this can reduce your cash outlay for assets (stuff) you purchase.

A loan taken out on a vehicle or other purchase is a cash flow positive because you are borrowing money to pay for whatever asset (stuff) you are purchasing rather than using your cash.

Principal payments on equipment or other loans is a cash flow negative because you are using your cash to lower the balance on your assets (stuff).

As you can see, there are a great many things that can positively or negatively impact your cash flow. A good understanding of this can mean the difference between staying in business and going out of business. It doesn't much matter what your year-end net profit is if you don't maintain a positive cash flow to stay in business.

Now that you know the basic fundamentals of a profit and loss statement and a balance sheet, and a little about cash flow, the next question is how to relate these to a specific business—and more important, how can you use them as an effective management tool.

Before you begin any business, it is imperative to do a realistic projected budget. Create a budget that is similar to the profit and loss statement example in this chapter using your best, most informed estimation of accurate numbers; this can be key to determining the possible success or failure of your business. It is unbelievable how many businesses begin without this important fundament. If you are planning on opening your own business, the single most important thing to do—and the very first thing you should do—is put together a preliminary budget with numbers that you are confident are extremely reasonable, well thought out, and accurate but conservative. The key numbers you must determine are (1) sales, (2) cost of goods sold as a percentage of sales, and (3) expenses. If your cost of goods and your expenses exceed your sales, it is mathematically impossible for your business to succeed!

What are your projected gross annual sales? This is not a number that you can afford to guess at; it is the basis for everything else you do in the planning of your business. If you don't have a solid and accurate number, you are not even close to starting your business. Do whatever research is necessary and possible to accurately determine this number. Talk to your accountant, get information from the small business administration, talk to other owners and managers of similar businesses and, if necessary, get a job in a similar business. If this number is wrong, everything else will be too.

What is your cost of goods sold? What are your direct costs? Do the math carefully. Find out what your product or service costs to produce. This too is a critical number, and you can't guess at it. What does the product you are selling cost you? This can also assist you in determining what your anticipated gross sales may be. If you are selling books, how much do you have to pay for an average book, if you are buying it in bulk and/or at wholesale? If you are paying five dollars for a book (your cost of goods sold), what are you able to sell that same book for and still be competitive? Suppose that you are able to sell each book for ten dollars; how many books will you have to sell to meet your projected sales figure, and is that a realistic number?

What are your expenses? What does it cost for you to stay in business? What is your payroll expected to be (including your own pay) and, if you need an office or a store front, what are all of the costs involved with that? What are your insurance costs, marketing and advertising costs, and any other miscellaneous costs that you will incur? Do a detailed calculation of all your anticipated expenses.

Once you have carefully determined these numbers, and so long as your cost of goods sold plus your expenses combined do not exceed your sales, you are ready for the next step.

If you have even a single penny in costs, it is mathematically impossible to make 100 percent profit. If you pay a penny for your product, and sell it for $10 million, the most your gross profit could be is; 99.9999 percent.

One of the most difficult equations that I had trouble understanding when I was learning accounting was markups and margins. I was under the same misconception that most people are: that if you mark something up 100 percent you'll then make 100 percent (gross profit). Leave expenses completely out of the equation, and only focus on cost of goods sold (direct costs). If you pay ten dollars for your product and you sell it for twenty dollars you may have marked it up 100 percent, but you actually only made 50 percent profit on it. The same math holds true if you are trying to achieve a 40 percent margin: you can't realize that by only marking up 40 percent; in fact, you would have to mark your costs up 67 percent in order to achieve a 40 percent margin.

Keep in mind that your percent of profit is based on a percent of your gross sales, and not on a percent of your cost of goods. If your business puts a 20 percent markup on whatever you sell, you might think that you are making a 20 percent margin, or a 20 percent profit; the reality is that you are actually only making a 16.7 percent profit ($100 x 1.2 = $120 x 16.7% = $20). Your profit in this example is $20 ($100 + 20% = $120), however 20 percent of $120 is $24, which is $4 more than the profit you received; $20 is only 16.7 percent of $120.

Once you understand markups and margins, you next need to determine what the markup on your product or service should be. First you need to know how much of a markup that the market will bear. In other words, if the cost of your product is $10, and the market retail price of that product is $13.50, then the market will dictate your markup to be 35 percent. Then the question is, can you sell enough of your product, at that markup to earn enough to cover all of your indirect costs and still make a reasonable profit? If you can't, your only other option is to determine whether to reduce your markup to below the industry standard, say to 30 percent, making the retail price of your product only $13.00; will that decrease in a retail price below that of your competition increase your likely gross sales to a number that will support your business (the Sam Walton theory)? This can be a dangerous decision because your competition may follow suit, and you will not only not get the gross revenue you need but also will be earning a lesser gross profit than what your business can sustain.

Moving the clock forward twenty-plus years from the time I first began my entrepreneurial endeavors, I can really appreciate the value and importance of accounting and knowing my numbers. After going through an intense IRS audit ten years previously that I came out of in good shape, my accountant and I found ourselves the target of another audit in 2009 for the previous three years (2006–8). I was confident that I didn't owe anything, and that I had paid every penny of taxes I owed, so I wasn't at all concerned. What I would have thought to be a fairly simple audit turned into a grueling examination of all my businesses with a magnifying glass.

At the time I was involved in multiple businesses collectively doing tens of millions of dollars a year in business. Unfortunately I found myself with an auditor who was less than experienced enough to do an audit as complicated as mine was, and may have had some ulterior motive to make a name for herself. More than two years later, after providing thousands of documents and expending tens of thousands of dollars in accounting fees, I got notification from the auditor that I owed the IRS a whopping sum of $987,000! That's right, nearly a million dollars, a sum that made the $30,000 tax liability I actually owed from my first year in business, look like peanuts!

It was around the beginning of 2011 that I received this notice; after just barely surviving the wrath of the Great Recession I now had the IRS telling me that I owed it almost a million dollars. The only good news was that I knew without a doubt that the IRS was wrong! For me to have owed a million dollars in taxes would have meant that I would have mis-reported about $4 million of income in a three-year period, and I knew that was impossible. Unfortunately it didn't matter that I knew it, or that my accountant knew it; we were dealing with an auditor who wouldn't admit to any mistakes or ignorance.

My accountant and I agreed that the only thing I could do was hire a tax attorney to file an appeal, which would move my case to a higher-level auditor and hopefully get someone who would take an objective look and who understood the complexity of my returns. A year later, the IRS wrote me a check for each of the three years in question. The total of the three checks was $63,000—the amount that I had *overpaid* in taxes for the three years they audited. Unbelievable, right? Knowing my numbers and sticking to my guns saved me over a million dollars. The IRS later admitted publically that they had targeted conservatives and conservative groups. I had previously written a conservative business column for a local business journal and suspect that I may have been targeted for that reason.

❭Action Steps

1. Write down your family budget; what is your total income and what are your total expenses; for each month and annually.

2. If you are in business, review your annual budget and make any adjustments necessary to ensure its accuracy.

3. Review your bank notes, or mortgages, identifying the terms, the interest rate, and the balance.

4. Make an action plan to reduce and eliminate your overall debt.

Knowing your numbers is important whether you are in business for yourself or just managing your family or personal finances. Start with the elementary steps; write down all of your expenses, being very detailed; then compare that to what your after-tax income is. Do this in both your personal life and your business. If what you're spending exceeds what you are bringing in, there is a definite problem that needs your immediate attention.

Make a note of each of these action steps, then prioritize completing each of them once you have finished this book.

CHAPTER EIGHT

Don't Drink the Kool-Aid

Don't drink the Kool-Aid. What does that mean? It means think for yourself. If you are going to have an opinion about anything, make damn sure it's an informed opinion! The only thing worse than having no opinion at all is having an uninformed opinion. Think for yourself, and don't be naive. If you are going to be successful in life, it's imperative that you deal only in facts. Seek out the truth, regardless of whether it's what you want to hear. Open your eyes to the truth and deal with it head on. If you have blinders on, take them off. Avoid tunnel vision at all costs. The truth shall set you free!

As the captain of your ship, you'd better be well informed with the facts, have a strong ability to think for yourself, and make your own decisions based on facts and experience, not on myth, tradition, or folklore. It took a good ship captain to discover that the world was round when it was commonly thought at the time that it was flat. That ship captain thought, if the world is flat, as everyone tells me, why is it that the first part of a ship you see as it approaches the port is the top of the mast? Reasonable deduction told him that the only way for that to happen was if the ocean wasn't level or flat as everyone thought; it meant that the world had to be round—otherwise one would see a full frontal view of a ship as it approached. Christopher Columbus had the intelligence and the confidence to question what people had told him was fact.

Understand the old adage that if something is too good to be true, it probably is. Think for yourself, trust your instincts; don't drink the Kool-Aid. Have you ever received some variation of an e-mail from a supposed Nigerian general or someone else telling you that there has been some sort of coup in his country, he is on the run from political persecution, needs to park $10 million in your bank account so he can safely get his money out of the country, and will give you part of it if you would just help him out? I'm here to tell you that there is some crook living high on the hog from all of the suckers who buy into such a ridiculous notion.

How about the people who believe that they've found their true love over the Internet, and often even get engaged without ever even meeting that person? We have to stop and ask ourselves, who could be that foolish or that naive? Actually, that's putting in nicely; who could possibly be that *stupid*?

You may remember the story back from January 2013 about the hoax that came to light; University of Notre Dame football star Manti Te'o had carried on a three-year online love affair with Stanford University student Lennay Keua. After Lennay was supposedly diagnosed with leukemia, Te'o told reporters that he phoned her every night in her hospital bed and prayed that she would return to health. As the story goes, Lennay died on September 12, 2012, just hours after Te'o's grandmother had also passed away. Three months later, on December 6, Te'o received a call from Lennay declaring that she was still alive and Te'o finally realized that he had been the victim of an elaborate hoax. As it turned out Lennay Keua was not a beautiful twenty-one-year-old woman dying from leukemia but a twenty-two-year-old man named Ronaiah Tuliasosopo, who had an admitted infatuation and attraction to Te'o. Tuliasosopo had used photographs of an old high school classmate,

Diane O'Meara, without her knowledge. By this time the entire world knew about Te'o's girlfriend, who had supposedly died of leukemia. Being a finalist for the Heisman Trophy, Te'o used some terrible judgment and briefly tried to carry on with the hoax that the love of his life had died of leukemia in a failed effort to avoid the embarrassment and humiliation. It all blew up in his face a month later when the story made national headlines in January 2013. Here was a guy with obvious talent and education who allowed himself to be tricked for an extended period of time. Manti Te'o wanted to believe it was all true, so he drank the Kool-Aid.

You may have seen the Lifetime TV movie of one of the most infamous online love affairs that ended in disaster; this time, however, the victims weren't nearly as lucky as Manti Te'o. This is the 2005 story of Talhotblond (tall hot blonde) meets Marinesniper (marine sniper). Thomas Montgomery, a married forty-six-year-old, began frequenting Internet chat rooms using the name Marinesniper and much younger photos of himself from his days in the military. He soon met Talhotblond, an eighteen-year-old named Jessi from West Virginia. Montgomery's wife soon discovered this online affair, confronted Jessi, and put an end to Thomas's deception. Outraged by the online actions of this middle-aged man, Jessi turned to Montgomery's coworker, twenty-two-year old Brian Barrett, who went by the name Beefcake. Jessi determined that she and Beefcake were a much better fit for each other and pursued a steamy online affair with Barrett. When Montgomery found out, he was so enraged that he shot and killed his coworker and disappeared in order to find Jessi and try to make amends with his true love. The police soon located Jessi to try and ensure the safety of the young woman; however they were astonished to find out that Talhotblond was actually a middle-aged housewife named Mary Sheiler who had been using her own daughter's photographs and pretending to be her. Sheiler's husband divorced her, and her daughter moved out. Montgomery plead guilty to murder and was sentenced to twenty years in prison. Talk about drinking the Kool-Aid! That drink cost one young man his life, and cost another man twenty years in prison.

The sad thing is that Sheiler, the one who caused all of this, didn't face any criminal prosecution.

In my many years of business, I've certainly ran into my share of liars and con artists; and I've developed a pretty good nose for sniffing them out. One of my businesses is a general real estate company (Millennium Realty Group, Inc.) which specializes in marketing and selling very high end luxury homes, more particularly luxury homes that my construction company designed and built. One particular type of liar I've ran into on multiple occasions; is the individual or "couple" who charade's around pretending that they; a) are in the market to purchase a luxury home, and b) that they can afford to purchase a luxury home. You might think of this as a fairly innocent or victimless prank; but try telling that to the realtor who's invested several days if not weeks showing properties to people they think are serious buyers. No doubt; shame on the gullible realtor who should have done a much better job at pre-qualifying their buyer. But, one tries to give everyone the benefit of the doubt, and tries not to judge a book by its cover; besides, as I've outlined in previous chapters in this book, you never know who you might be dealing with. Moreover; people want to believe, they want to believe so badly that they don't trust their instincts or their experience. That realtor wants to sell a multi-million dollar house so bad, and can only concentrate on that big commission they hope to earn, that they don't listen to that voice in the back of their heads that is telling them that there is no way that this "buyer" is for real. Besides, why on earth would anyone carry on such a ridiculous charade if it wasn't true? Ask any realtor who specializes in selling high end homes, and they will tell you that it's not at all uncommon. Why would people carry on such a game? Who knows, most likely because they have nothing better to do, and pretending like they can afford a luxury home, is probably similar to dreaming about winning the lottery to some people. The moral of this story is to trust your experience and trust your instincts, and if you are investing your time or money, make sure you know and verify who it is that you are dealing with.

Having been in business all of my adult life, I've just about seen it all. Not drinking the Kool-Aid doesn't simply stop at not being naive or gullible; it's a whole state of mind, a whole confidence that you aren't going to buy anyone's bullshit, no matter who's peddling it or how sweet it might all sound. It's an affirmation to yourself that you are going to be your own person and you are going to make up your own mind about what matters in life. It's a determination that you are going to stay informed on the things that really matter in the world, and in your life, so that you have an informed opinion.

They say that it's never a good idea to talk about sports, politics, or religion. OK then, what else is there? Just kidding. Since all three topics are quite relative to drinking the Kool-Aid, we can't get past this chapter without addressing them. I'm going to step out on a real limb here and try to talk a little bit about all three topics, and try not to offend anyone in the process. OK, let's get sports out of the way: I'm a diehard Kansas City Chiefs fan, and don't much keep up on many sports other than football. Even when the Chiefs have had a long run of bad luck, I have always remained a steadfast and loyal fan; so I have drunk the Kool-Aid season after season, believing in my team because I want it so badly to be true: I want to believe that my team will once again be Super Bowl champions!

Politics and religion are tougher topics, because most people in this country have strong and often very different beliefs on both. In the case of politics, at least, you have about a third of the country who leans conservative or republican, another third of the country who leans liberal or democrat, and the other third of the country who usually decides most elections who identify themselves as right in the middle or independent. It would certainly be much easier to avoid this topic altogether for the purposes of this book; but when you are having a serious conversation about not drinking the Kool-Aid you can't have it without including religion and politics, because when most people drink the Kool-Aid it quite often has something to do with one or the other—and sometimes both.

I'm a Christian and I believe in heaven and hell. I'm far from perfect, and have made my share of mistakes along my journey, but I do make every effort to live my life in a manner that I hope will leave me with little explaining to do whenever I finally meet my maker. That said, I have little time for those who wear their religion on their sleeves.

Religion no doubt brings a lot of good to a lot of people's lives. It has also unfortunately been used to brainwash and manipulate lesser-minded people throughout history. In fact, most wars since the beginning of time have been fought in the name of religion. As the song "One Tin Soldier" goes, "Do it in the name of heaven, so you can justify it in the end."

As regards politics, full disclosure: I'm a constitutional and fiscal conservative and "lean" libertarian (limited government). I have developed my own informed opinion of my political positions over many years based on what I have determined is best for me, my family, my business, and what I think is the best course for the country I live in. That said, I'm the first to admit that there are a lot of unscrupulous, and sometimes downright stupid, politicians on both sides of the aisle. As a business owner, an entrepreneur, a capitalist, and a believer in limited government and American exceptionalism, I couldn't in good conscious be anything other than a conservative. As I mentioned earlier in this book, there are ten words you never want to hear: "I am from the government, and I'm here to help." Don't drink the Kool-Aid!

Whatever your politics, know what your positions are on the issues, and do your own homework. Always look at and listen to both sides of the issues. Something that may sound like a great idea in theory may have unintended consequences that might not be so good. A fifteen dollar minimum wage, for example, sounds great in theory, and no doubt if you're making less than that amount it sounds like a really great idea! But is it such a great idea if it forces your employer out of business or causes him to lay off half of his workforce, and you find yourself out of a job? What about the products a business sells? What if an increased payroll forces the business to double the cost of what it's selling to cover its increased costs, and customers won't pay for the increase? That could quickly put the company out of business, and that certainly wouldn't be good for anyone. So think things through, and consider the consequences. Don't buy into what at first glimpse might seem to be a good idea until you have completely considered all of the consequences.

Never forget that there is no such thing as a free lunch. Those who are getting a free lunch don't much care who's paying for it so long as it keeps being free. But what happens when the guy who's paying for the free lunch suddenly quits paying for whatever reason? Those getting the free lunch have become dependent, and suddenly finds that they are unable to fend for themselves.

I've shared my thoughts, beliefs, and positions on religion and politics to encourage you to ask yourself where you stand on the issues. I truly believe that your politics become part of who you are, especially if you are in business, so you had better take the time to know and understand your politics. It's not something that you need to know the answers to immediately (unless you are getting ready to vote); in fact, if you aren't sure what a political party's platform is, you shouldn't make any decision until you do some serious research and find the answers to some or all of your questions.

People often develop their religious or political beliefs because of their upbringing, heritage, or their culture. I'm suggesting that you look beyond that, keeping your upbringing and heritage as part of the equation in your deliberation, maybe even 49 percent of it, but not all of it. Think for yourself. I'm a Christian because I was raised that way, and I have faith in a higher purpose; but so long as people of faith, whatever that faith is, believe in peace and goodwill toward others, they will never hear a religious sermon out of me. I'm a conservative because of my personal positions, and what I think is best for me, my family, my business and this country. People of goodwill can have legitimate disagreements, and debate the issues; that is what makes our democracy great. We can agree to disagree, and respect one another's positions, so long as we educate ourselves on our positions, to ensure ourselves of an informed opinion.

One could obviously write an entire library of books on sports, religion and politics, and many already have. I certainly have some strong convictions with regards to my politics, but we will leave that commentary for another book, other than to say I'm a an entrepreneur, and a capitalist; I believe in working hard each and every day, creating jobs and opportunities, and—yes, call me crazy, call me greedy, call me whatever you like—I believe in creating a better place in life for me and my family, and creating wealth and financial security for our future. Isn't that what being an entrepreneur is all about—making a better life for ourselves and our family? Isn't that really the American dream?

Hopefully by now you have a pretty good grasp on what "Don't drink the Kool-Aid" means: think for yourself, don't be a follower, don't have tunnel vision, have an informed opinion, and see things as they really are. Don't rationalize away all of the red flags or alarm bells going off in your brain. Trust your gut feeling, your instincts and intuition.

I'm going to go a little off the reservation here, and tell a few short stories of how large groups of people have been brainwashed into doing some very horrific things to others and themselves simply because they wanted to believe what some charismatic con artist was telling them. I think these stories are important to include in this chapter not only because they are an important part of our history but also because there is a valuable lesson in thinking for ourselves that can be learned from our history.

History has taught us a hard lesson over and over about the dangers of not thinking clearly for ourselves. Sense the beginning of time, there have been hundreds if not thousands of real events that have taken place that have cost millions of human lives due to people just following along and not thinking for themselves. During World War II, Nazi Germany—led by Adolf Hitler—initiated a program of systematic state-sponsored murder, resulting in the death of six million Jews, including one million children and two million women. Hitler believed the German bloodline was a superior race, and somehow convinced the masses of his population that it was OK to commit genocide to preserve that superior race. Holocaust historian Christopher Browning, in his book *Ordinary Men*, argues that ordinary people can kill out of obedience to authority and peer pressure and not just bloodlust or hatred. When ordinary people are placed in a cohesive group, most will obey commands given by an authoritative figure who is seen as legitimate even if they find those commands to be morally reprehensible. In other words, they fail to think for themselves, and they just go along.

You don't have to go as far back as the 1940s, to find similar stories of tragedy, initiated by charismatic leaders who brainwash large groups of people to do the unthinkable. There are many similar stories even in our lifetime. You may have been asking yourself when you started reading this chapter where the expression "Don't drink the Kool-Aid" comes from. The expression originated because of one man's ability to impose his political and religious agenda on nearly a thousand people, so much so that he was able to get them and their children to willingly drink Kool-Aid that they knew was poisoned with cyanide, even as they witnessed people who drank before them dying in agony.

Perhaps you remember this experiment in socialism that ended in tragedy in the late 1970s It was carried out by a guy named Jim Jones, who used to rub elbows with prominent politicians of the time, such as California governor Jerry Brown, vice president Walter Mondale, and first lady Rosalynn Carter; he was even instrumental in getting San Francisco mayor George Moscone elected in 1975. Jones enjoyed public support from some of the highest-level politicians in the United States.

Jones had previously formed the Peoples Temple, which practiced what it called *apostolic socialism*. Eventually the press started reporting that the Peoples Temple was moving even further to the left of the mainstream in its embrace of socialism, which resulted in some harsh criticism of Jones and his followers.

In 1974 Jones and the Peoples Temple negotiated with the Guyanese Government a lease of over 3,800 acres of land in north-western Guyana and moved the Peoples Temple there. This property was named Jonestown after Jim Jones himself; the formal name was the Peoples Temple Agricultural Project.

Jonestown became notorious worldwide, when on November 18, 1978, 918 people died in the settlement, as well as at a nearby airstrip, and in Georgetown, Guyana's capital. As Wikipedia notes, "A total of 909 Temple members died in Jonestown, all but two from apparent cyanide poisoning, in an event termed as 'revolutionary suicide' as outlined by Jones and some other members in an audio tape of the event and in prior discussions. The poisonings in Jonestown followed the murder of five others by Temple members at Port Kaituma [a nearby airstrip], including US Congressman Leo Ryan. Four others died in Georgetown at Jones' command." Congressman Ryan had traveled to Jonestown to investigate accusations that some members were being held against their will and were forced to turn their welfare checks over to Jones and the Peoples Temple. According to Wikipedia, "Up to $65,000 in monthly payments from U.S. government agencies to Jonestown residents were signed over to the Temple."

Wikipedia also notes, "To an extent, the actions in Jonestown were viewed as a mass suicide; some sources, including Jonestown survivors, regard the event as a mass murder. It was the largest such event in modern history and resulted in the largest single loss of American civilian life in a deliberate act until the events of September 11, 2001."

Prior to the tragic events, Temple members had practiced what were referred to as "White Nights" during which a "revolutionary suicide" vote was taken of the members to simulate a mass suicide rehearsal. Peoples Temple defector Deborah Layton described the event in an affidavit:

> "Everyone, including the children, was told to line up. As we passed through the line, we were given a small glass of red liquid to drink. We were told that the liquid contained poison and that we would die within 45 minutes. We all did as we were told. When the time came when we should have dropped dead, Rev. Jones explained that the poison was not real and that we had just been through a loyalty test. He warned us that the time was not far off when it would become necessary for us to die by our own hands."

A forty-four-minute cassette tape, known as the "death tape," recorded much of the events of the evening, including aides preparing a large metal tub filled with Flavor Aid and poisoned with Valium, chloral hydrate, cyanide, and Phenergan. On the tape, Jones urged Temple members to commit "revolutionary suicide," which was explained as the theory that "you could go down in history saying you chose your own way to go, and it is your commitment to refuse capitalism and in support of socialism." No dissent could be heard on the tape. As Wikipedia notes, "According to escaped Temple member Odell Rhodes, the first to take the poison were Ruletta Paul and her one-year-old infant. A syringe with its needle removed was used to squirt poison into the infant's mouth and then Paul squirted another syringe into her own mouth. Jonestown member Stanley Clayton "also saw mothers with their babies first approach the table containing the poison" and said that "Jones approached people to encourage them to drink the poison." After others saw the horrific reactions of the poison taking effect, Jones counseled, "Die with a degree of dignity... I tell you, I don't care how many screams you hear, I don't care how many anguished cries...death is a million times preferable to ten more days of this life."

Jones was later found dead lying next to his chair, with his head cushioned by a pillow; his death was caused by a gunshot wound to his left temple, and a coroner later determined that it was consistent with a self-inflicted gunshot wound. It seemed Jones didn't drink his own Kool-Aid, and took the quick coward's way out by putting a bullet in his head. In 1978 the Temple's wealth was estimated to be approximately $26 million. Typewritten notes were found signed by Marceline Jones (Jim Jones's wife), along with other Temple members, leaving all of their assets to the Communist Party of the USSR; the letters included information on assets and bank accounts.

Fifteen years after the Jonestown massacre, US law enforcement authorities found themselves facing another tragedy at the hands of another fanatical religious group calling themselves the Branch Davidians. They were led by David Koresh (aka Vernon Howell), a charismatic self-proclaimed prophet who convinced his people that if they believed in him he would take them to the promised-land. On February 28, 1993 US Alcohol, Tobacco, and Firearms agents attempted to serve a warrant for weapons violations on the group, at their Mount Carmel compound just outside of Waco, Texas. An intense gun battle ensued that resulted in the death of four federal Agents and six Branch Davidians. The failed raid resulted in a fifty-one-day standoff, which ended on April 19 when the Federal Bureau of Investigation launched an assault that included a tear gas attack in an attempt to force the Branch Davidians out. A fire engulfed the Mount Carmel compound killing seventy-six men, women, and children, including Koresh himself. An investigation in 2000 concluded that the members themselves had started the fire at the time of the attack.

On September 11, 2001, nineteen Muslim extremists hijacked four passenger airliners and brutally attacked America. Two of the planes, American Airlines flight 11, and United Airlines flight 175, were crashed into the north and south towers of the World Trade Center in New York City. Within two hours, both towers collapsed. A third plane, American

Airlines flight 77, was crashed into the Pentagon. A fourth plane, United Airlines flight 93, was targeted at Washington, D.C., but crashed in a field near Shanksville, Pennsylvania, after the passengers—who via cell phones had already heard about the world Trade Center and Pentagon attacks—tried to overcome the terrorists and take back control of the plane. In all, 2,977 people lost their lives, as did the nineteen hijackers. US intelligence quickly concluded that the attacks were launched by the terrorist group al-Qaeda, led by Osama bin Laden.

The attack on 9/11 was the worse tragedy on American soil since the Civil War. America responded by attacking al-Qaeda training camps in Afghanistan, a war ensued that lasted over twelve years. Having evaded capture for years, bin Laden was located in a compound in Pakistan and killed by US Navy Seals in May 2011.

Al-Qaeda launched what it referred to as a holy war against America on 9/11, doing so for religious and political reasons. The group justified its actions because of US involvement in previous conflicts involving Muslims, US support of Israel, and US involvement in Saudi Arabia. The 9/11 hijackers definitely drank the Kool-Aid; bin Laden had promised them eternal life, with a thousand virgin wives, and they flew planes into buildings because they wanted to believe him.

OK, some of these stories may be a little over the top for a motivational book, but if your goal is to be successful in life, you can't be naive in the process. I feel that these stories are good examples to demonstrate just how important it is that you think for yourself. If history has taught us anything, it's that people desperately want to believe, and often overlook all sense of reason in the process. Jim Jones, David Koresh, and Osama bin Laden were no different from Adolf Hitler or Josef Stalin; they were all charismatic leaders, and their followers wanted to believe so badly that they drank whatever Kool-Aid was put in front of them.

One has to ask, what could possibly cause a human being to give up all deductive reasoning? How could people permit themselves to carry on an Internet relationship with a fictitious person they have never met? How do you convince someone to fly a jet into a building? Worse yet, how could parents allow themselves and their children to be brainwashed to the point that they willingly are subjected to poisoning or burned to death? The answer is that they desperately wanted to believe, so they drank the Kool-Aid. It happens much more often than you would think, and more than most would admit. It happens every day; hearts are broken, fortunes are lost, people are killed, and bad leaders are elected because people have blinders on, and they want to believe so badly that they lose all reasonable thought, and they drink the Kool-Aid.

You've probably already had dozens if not hundreds of people in your lifetime try to hustle you, con you, or just down right bullshit you. Think about it; how often has it happened, and how many times have you fallen for it, even though all intelligent thought tried to keep you from doing it? I'm not just talking about all the people you have known that are just downright liars, and bloviate whatever they have to say to make themselves look better or more important. I'm talking about people who have conned you out of money, or hustled you out of your britches or—worse yet—your heart. Listen to the alarm bells; don't drink the Kool-Aid!

First and foremost, be honest with yourself. If you can't be honest with yourself you are in serious trouble, because there is nothing worse than drinking your own Kool-Aid. People do it—you know what I'm talking about. That is the most pathetic situation—when someone actually convinces themselves of their own BS.

Think for yourself! If you have blinders on, take them off! Avoid tunnel vision at all costs! If something is too good to be true, it most likely is. Don't drink the Kool-Aid!

)Action Steps

1. Identify three times in your personal life that you have been deceived, tricked, or fooled. Then identify the personal and/or monetary damages you incurred because of this deceit.

2. Identify three times in your professional or business life that you have been deceived, tricked, or fooled. Then identify the personal and/or monetary damages you incurred because of this deceit.

3. Ask yourself what you would do differently in hindsight.

4. What are your political views, and why do you hold these particular views?

5. Have a self-evaluation, and make sure you see things the way they really are. Avoid tunnel vision at all costs.

In order to learn from our mistakes and misjudgments it is important that we first recognize them. Clearly understanding our politics, and our convictions, can often give us a reality check on what's going on in the world around us.

Write down your responses to these action steps before you move on to the next chapter. If you aren't completely certain of your political views, take the time necessary to develop an informed opinion.

CHAPTER NINE

Own It

Again, the "*it*" is everything in life. Take responsibility; don't pass the buck or put the blame off on someone else. It's a question of character; do you have it, or not? If you have good character, you own every situation, you take responsibility for your actions. If you pass the blame off onto others, you probably need to take a really good look at yourself and your character and then reevaluate both.

You are the captain of your ship; you are responsible for everything on board. If you hit an iceberg at sea, *you* hit the iceberg; it didn't hit you. You didn't navigate around it. If someone else is driving the ship while you are putting out a fire in the engine room and that person runs the ship aground, guess what, *you* still own it! You either didn't put the right person at the helm of the ship or you didn't properly train that person to take over in your absence. If your ship sinks, remember that you alone are the captain; it's your responsibility and yours alone to keep your ship out of harm's way and keep it afloat! If it gets torpedoed by another ship; what did you do to put your ship in harm's way, or what didn't you do to adequately protect your ship? If you run into a typhoon, are you an experienced enough captain to navigate through it or circumvent it all together? If your ship is taking on water, it's your job to pump it out and repair the leak. Blaming your crew, the rough waters, another ship, or Mother Nature will get you nothing but sunk! As the captain of your ship you are also responsible for the safety and welfare of your crew and cargo. The buck stops with you! If you don't reach the destination you want in life, you have no one to blame but yourself.

Speaking of ship captains, Captain Francesco Schettino is an example that comes to mind of a captain who *didn't* own it, didn't take responsibility for himself, his crew, or his passengers. You may recall the disaster involving the luxury Italian cruise ship *Costa Concordia* that run aground at Isola del Giglio on January 13, 2012, when it hit a reef while doing an unofficial near-shore salute to the local islanders. The ship partially sank while carrying 4,254 passengers, thirty-two of whom lost their lives and two of whom were never accounted for.

Having lost control of his ship, Captain Schettino did nothing to contact the nearby harbor for assistance but merely tried to resume course, before he finally had to turn back to Giglio. After an hour of listing and drifting, and the captain's assertions that the incident was only part of a small technical failure, he finally had to order an evacuation. Meanwhile, the harbor authorities were being alerted by worried passengers.

Maritime law has long dictated that the captain of a ship must be the last person off a sinking ship, and may never abandon ship until all passengers and crew are safely off the ship; it's the captain's ultimate responsibility! Captain Schettino must have been absent the day that lesson was taught. While the ship was still in peril with hundreds of passengers still aboard in desperate need of assistance, and all of the passengers and crew still needing their captain, Schettino had found himself a nice safe spot on a lifeboat. In a phone call from the coast guard to Schettino, Captain Gregorio Maria De Falco repeatedly ordered Schettino to return to the ship from his lifeboat and take charge of the ongoing passenger evacuation. At one point in the call, De Falco grew so angry at Schettino's stalling that he raised his voice and told Schettino, "Vada a bardo, cazzo!" ("Get the f–k back on board, you dick!")

It's not a wonder that with the cowardly way that Captain Schettino abandoned ship, leaving his passengers and crew to fend for themselves, he would ultimately blame the shipwreck on everyone but himself. Schettino was charged with manslaughter, causing the shipwreck, and abandoning ship while passengers were still aboard. Instead of taking responsibility for his actions, he was quick to blame his crew and claimed that his helmsman waited thirteen seconds to move the tiller. He told the court, "If it weren't for [his] error, to not position the tiller to the left, the swerve [towards the rock] and the collision would not have happened." There's no doubt that if the captain had taken immediate responsibility and owned the situation by taking charge, there may have been a much better outcome, and he may have saved the lives of all of his passengers.

This is your life—you own it! Once you are an adult, you are 100 percent responsible for yourself and your actions. There is no more blaming Mom and Dad for whatever they did wrong or didn't do right. Life has dealt you whatever hand you have, and you own it. It's up to you and only you to change whatever you don't like about your life for the better. Don't waste any time dwelling on why you can't do something, or listing all the reasons you can't make it happen; focus instead on one reason why you can make it happen. Once you have realized one reason you can do something, the second and third reasons will quickly follow.

Winners accept responsibility, and losers blame everyone but themselves. I mean, why take responsibility when you can blame your parents, your employer, your siblings, your coworkers, your spouse, or your predecessor? You can't fix a problem until you first take responsibility for it, own it.

"Let's roll!" Those two words have become synonymous with individuals who take responsibility and own the situation. On the fateful morning of September 11, 2001, four terrorists boarded United Airlines flight 93, on its daily scheduled flight from Newark, New Jersey, to San Francisco. Approximately forty-six minutes into the flight, the hijackers breached the aircraft's cockpit and overpowered the flight crew. Terrorist Ziad Jarrah, a trained pilot, then took control of the aircraft and diverted it back toward the east coast of the United States in the direction of Washington, D.C., with a specific target believed to be the US Capitol.

After the hijackers took control of the plane, several passengers and flight attendants were able to make telephone calls and learned that attacks had already been made by other hijacked planes on the World Trade Center in New York City and the Pentagon outside of Washington, D.C. Realizing the gravity of the situation, some of the passengers attempted to regain control of the aircraft and stormed the cockpit. During the attempt, however, the plane lost control and crashed in a field in Stonycreek Township near Shanksville, Pennsylvania.

Flight recorders recovered from the crash site revealed how the brave actions taken by the passengers prevented the aircraft from reaching the hijackers' intended target, and likely saving thousands of people. The brave passengers on United flight 93 owned the situation they were in, saved thousands of lives in doing so, and effectively launched the first retaliatory strike against the terrorists who attacked our nation on 9/11.

We all know people who continuously pass the buck or don't take responsibility. It's always someone else's fault. Kids who blame their teachers, adults who still blame their parents, coworkers who blame their employers, and politicians who blame their predecessors. It's a terrible character flaw that can cripple people's ability to ever achieve greatness or genuine success in their lives.

I remember an incident that happened to me as a contractor several years ago. I was having what I thought was a private telephone conversation with one of my job foremen who was running a reconstruction project for a very difficult customer. This customer had run the previous contractor off the job for what I later discovered to be no good reason. At every turn, this customer continued to interfere and cause unnecessary problems, which continued to cost me time and money on the job. I commented to my job foreman, who had been with me for the past ten years, "Our customer is the craziest, most unreasonable person we've ever dealt with," among other comments communicated in frustration. No sooner did I get off the phone with my job foreman than he called me back a few minutes later. As it turned out, our difficult customer had been eavesdropping on our conversation and was obviously irate about our comments. No sooner did I get off the phone with my job foreman than I received a phone call from the insurance adjuster who was involved with the project and had just received an earful from our customer. What could I do? Own it! It was my comment, there was no getting around it; I had a furious customer, and it was my responsibility to deal with it head on.

I immediately drove to the jobsite, and headed straight for our irate customer. "I owe you an apology," I said, to which the customer immediately responded, "Oh yes, you sure do, buster." I then replied, "I would appreciate it if you would hear me out," and the customer gave me a somber look. I then replied, "I apologize that you heard the private conversation I was having with a trusted member of my management team; however, I have nothing to apologize for regarding the content of my conversation. Whether or not you would admit it to me, I have little doubt that you realize that you have been very difficult to deal with on this project, and that started long before I or my company showed up. I regret that you are dealing with this unwanted disaster that happened to your property, but we are here to rebuild it and help get your life and business back on track. If you want us to pack up and leave, we will do that right now, and I will refer you to another qualified contractor to finish this project for you. My team has been doing a great job here for you every day, and if you wish for us to stay and finish this project we will gladly do so, but we will not stay here if you intend to continue interfering with our progress." That comment left my customer with little if any response. She apologized, acknowledged that she had been difficult to deal with, and asked me if we would please stay and finish the job. Before I left the site, things were smoother than they had ever been, and as I left, the customer even complimented me on my staff and their good work.

While I was driving back to my office, the insurance adjuster who had just had his head bit off a couple hours earlier called me back and asked me what on earth I was able to say to completely turn the situation around. I simply responded, "I owned the situation." This was an adjuster that I had only done a little work for in the past, but from that day forward, I received every job that insurance adjuster ever got.

Imagine the different outcome had I simply buried my head in the sand and not even answered the phone when the adjuster called me to ask what happened. Or worse yet, had I denied that I ever said any such thing, thereby calling my customer a liar—that probably wouldn't have worked out too well. Or I could have pushed all the blame off on my job foreman and said that I was only responding to his frustrated comments. Any one of those reactions to that difficult situation may have been a standard option to someone who doesn't take responsibility, and all of them would have ended up disastrously! Sure, my response could have ended badly as well; the customer could have become more irate and thrown us off the property. If that would have happened, it would have been unfortunate, but it was an outcome that I could have lived with. It's seldom the act that gets you in trouble; it's your actions after the act, or the cover-up, that does the most damage.

While I'm telling my "own it" stories, there was one incident that happened for which I did everything I could, not to have to own it; it was the one time I would have gladly buried my head in the sand, if I could have only figured out how to do so. This story is slightly off point, but a story worth telling none the less. Several years ago, I was doing reconstruction for a client whose home had experienced significant fire loss. The client was a prominent psychiatrist and therapist with her own radio talk show, and had a mannerism akin to that of Dr. Ruth Westheimer. The good doctor was a bit difficult, to say the least, as many people are when they find themselves having suffered any kind of disaster in their home or business.

We had only been working on this particular job for a day or two, and I had our cleaning technicians there packing up the client's belongings so that we could bring them back to our warehouse and cleaning facility while we were rebuilding her house. I had a scheduled meeting at the house with "Dr. Ruth" that day so we could go over any changes she might want made to the house during our reconstruction process.

A few seconds prior to my walking in the front door with the home owner, one of my employees thought it might be funny to roll a vibrator they had discovered in her bedroom nightstand down the hardwood steps while it was turned on. Needless to say, as "Dr. Ruth" and I were walking in the door of her home, her vibrator came buzzing and bouncing down the hardwood steps as three or four of my employees convulsed with laughter at something that turned out to be *not* at all funny.

Any ideas on how you would talk or think your way out of that situation? Me neither. Firing all of the employees on the spot would have only drawn more attention to the situation, not to mention the fact they really didn't intend any malice, and it might have even been funny had I not been walking in the door with the homeowner at that instant. All I could do was pretend that I didn't see it and immediately move the homeowner into another room. It was an icy meeting, to say the least, and a terrible way to start a new project. Yes, that was the one time in my life that I wish I could have buried my head in the sand.

I previously addressed the hardships of divorce on a business (in chapter 2), and I learned that hard lesson firsthand. My divorce several years ago caused all of my cash reserve and my line of credit to be frozen, which made it difficult— almost impossible—to keep my business afloat, not to mention keeping my suppliers and subcontractors current; I mean what bank is going to lend anyone money when they have no idea how the outcome of a divorce will impact a business or the business owner. It didn't take long before I started to get behind on my payables, which as anyone in business understands is a very real and immediate problem. With the volume of business I was doing at the time, it wasn't uncommon to have a million dollars in current payables due at any given time, and this particular time was no different. Pretty soon I wasn't able to keep current, and the phone calls started coming in.

Every business owner who has been in business for any extended period of time has been in a similar cash flow situation at one time or another. It's a terrible place to be, and it can easily result in causing the business owner to freeze up and lose his or her ability to function effectively. Sometimes the path of least resistance is to bury your head in the sand and hope that the situation goes away. Believe me, it won't go away; no problem ever fixes itself. My initial reaction when I found myself in this situation was to panic, but fortunately I immediately realized that burying my head in the sand wouldn't solve anything and would only make matters worse.

So what do you do when it seems you are facing impossible odds? You own it, deal with it head on. What could I do? I was stuck between a rock and a hard place; you can't spend what you don't have. These were circumstances that were beyond my immediate control. Fortunately I had a long and good working relationship with most of my suppliers and subcontractors, so the only thing I could do was to talk to them and level with them. I personally contacted all of them, many in person; I explained the situation and worked out a payment schedule with each of them, breaking their balance into twelve equal payments. I then expressed that

I valued our business relationship and that I wanted to continue doing business with them, and that I understood if they didn't want to do further business with my company until this was resolved.

The response was overwhelmingly positive! Sure, there were a few who were mad and threw a fit, but the overwhelming response was that they were glad to at least know what the deal was and to know what they could expect. In all honesty it made my business relationship stronger with most of them, because they had all been through rough times themselves and were glad to hear firsthand that I would work through things with them when times got tough. In almost every instance, all of my subs and suppliers were happy to continue working with me. Fortunately this dilemma only lasted a couple of months; then my divorce was finalized and everything went back to normal.

I could have done what many would be tempted to do: avoid phone calls and bury my head in the sand. That would have ended up in disaster, likely running me out of business in a hurry. What I did was creatively develop a million-dollar line of credit for a period of time by simply working with my subcontractors and suppliers. I quickly recognized that all of these people that I was dealing with were businesspeople no different from me; I asked myself how I would want to be dealt with if I were in their position. This was an easy question for me to answer, because I had been in their position dozens of times, if not hundreds of times, with people who owed me money that I had a hard time collecting. You can always deal with the facts, and that is what everyone really wanted to know: What are the facts? Am I going to get paid, and if so, when? They all understood that it was much better to cooperate and work through this with one another than to be adversarial.

Leadership is all about taking responsibility. A leader who passes the buck or blames others is no leader at all. A leader understands that the buck stops with him- or herself and no one else. A leader always deals in facts and truths, not excuses or lies. Things happen in life; they're sometimes bad things or unintended things, but they happen. A leader takes ownership of anything he or she is responsible for—not just directly responsible but also remotely responsible. If I or my company makes a commitment to anyone I own it, regardless of whether someone else down the chain is the one who actually drops the ball. Obviously, if someone down my chain drops the ball, that person is going to have to own it *to me*; but I own it to everyone else. If my customer asks me why our company missed a deadline or went over budget, I take full responsibility, apologize, and offer a reasonable remedy to the solution. I don't offer excuses or blame it on one of the possibly weaker links in my organization. I own it with our customer and resolve it. Then, if there is a weaker link or a problem that caused us to miss our deadline, I deal with it internally.

It's amazing the positive response you will receive when you simply take responsibility, when you own it. Think about it: how many times in your own life have you been aggravated or even mad at an individual or a company you do business with because no one will take responsibility for whatever legitimate grievance you might have? It's amazing how far saying, "It's my responsibility, I apologize, and what can I do to make it right?" will get you. Nine times out of ten it takes all of the steam out of the customer's frustration or aggravation. It is hard to continue any argument with that kind of a response, and it is certainly hard to stay aggravated at someone who takes responsibility and owns the situation, especially if it is followed up with an apology and an offer to remedy it. That kind of response can simply and quickly turn aggravation into appreciation, because someone has acknowledged the issue and accepted responsibility. At that point, any further debate is usually moot.

You can't simply appoint someone to be a leader; they either have what it takes to be leaders or they don't. They either have the ability to inspire people to follow them or they don't. If you were in battle, who would you want to be stuck in a foxhole with—someone who is complaining and blaming everyone else in the world for his or her predicament, or someone who owns the situation, faces it head on and battles his or her way out? A leader doesn't necessarily have to be the one who holds the superior rank or title. A leader is the one who takes responsibility and takes charge of any given situation. The leader in battle isn't necessarily the general; it's often the private who inspires everyone by grabbing the flag and charging up the hill, screaming, "Let's take this freaking hill!" as everyone else follows in the charge.

My favorite "captain Story" is the story of Captain Chesley B. "Sully" Sullenberger, a former US Air Force fighter pilot. You might say that Captain Sullenberger is the opposite of Captain Schettino of the Italian cruise ship *Costa Concordia* (discussed previously in this chapter).

On January 15, 2009, US Airways flight 1549 was leaving La Guardia Airport in New York City. The Airbus A320-214 had just taken off on its route when it struck a flock of Canadian geese during its initial climb; it lost engine power, and this forced an emergency landing on the Hudson River just off Midtown Manhattan.

The bird strike occurred just three minutes into the flight and resulted in an immediate and complete loss of thrust from both engines. Captain Sullenberger communicated his situation with the flight control tower, and he was instructed to attempt to reach an airstrip in Teterboro, New Jersey. With a clear understanding of his aircraft's condition, he made a command decision and replied to the traffic control tower that he was landing in the Hudson. Captain Sullenberger took responsibility and owned the situation. In a calm voice he announced to the crew and passengers, "Prepare for impact."

"He was phenomenal," passenger Joe Hart said, "He landed it—I tell you what—the impact wasn't a whole lot more than a rear-end collision. It threw you into the seat ahead of you. Both engines cut out and he actually floated it into the river." As another passenger described it,

"It was intense. It was intense. You've got to give it to the pilot. He made a hell of a landing."

Witnesses said the plane's pilot appeared to simply guide the plane down. Bob Read, a television producer who saw the crash from his office window, said it appeared to be a controlled descent.

All 150 passengers and five crew members were safely rescued from the wings of the airliner that rested in the icy waters of the Hudson River on a twenty-degree day. Captain "Sully" Sullenberger was the last one to exit the plane. This is a real-life story of an American hero who took control of a terrible situation and "made it happen." He took responsibility for the situation; he owned it.

If you want to achieve real success in your life, you must first take ownership of your life, and your actions.

❯Action Steps

1. Identify any unresolved issues in your personal life that you should take ownership of today. What are you waiting for? This may be the only invitation you get to take ownership!

2. Identify the three best things that you have done for other individuals—things that might be considered heroic. Be specific.

3. Identify the three best things that other individuals have done for you in your life—things that might be considered heroic. Be specific.

Take ownership of your life. Anything that happened before today can't be changed, but you can take ownership of it. Take responsibility for your past and your present, make every effort to resolve any unresolved issues, then put the past behind you and look toward the future. Make a conscious decision to take responsibility for everything in your life from this day forward.

Write down your responses to these action steps before moving on to the next chapter.

CHAPTER TEN

Life Is Short

Life is short; don't miss out on it. Don't put off until tomorrow what you could and should do today. Make a decision to "make it happen"; make your life happen the way you want it to. Live your life to the fullest, and without any regrets. It is never too soon or too late to get an education, start a business, or do what you want in life. Time flies by in the blink of an eye; are you going to enjoy the life you've dreamed of, or wish you'd done things a lot differently?

You are the captain of your ship; your mission in life is to define your destiny, to set course on life's journey, and for you and your cargo to safely reach your destination. Enjoy the journey, and make life be what you want it to be!

If you own a business, never lose track of the reason you went into business for yourself. What was it you wanted out of your business—independence, financial security, or to be your own boss? Always remember that "business is only a tool to help you get what you want out of life." Run your business, don't let it run you. If your business is running you, I seriously doubt you are getting out of it, what it was that caused you to go into business for yourself for in the first place.

Don't sweat the small stuff! Life is too short to sweat the little things, and to dwell over that which we can't change. Do you ever stop and think about how much time in your life has been wasted away fretting over the little things? At the end of the day they usually don't make a bit of difference. How about the people who just have to be right no matter what? How much of their life do you think they spend trying to convince themselves or others that they are right, and does that really matter in the long run? Do you want to be right, or do you want to be happy?

There's no time like the present. I once had a business associate I had contemplated entering into a partnership with who used to profess how patient he was. You might say he wore it like a badge of honor. There is nothing wrong with being patient; but I soon realized that my friend was a procrastinator. You can overanalyze things to death, and opportunities can quickly be lost. Some of the best deals I ever lost were lost by only one day's delay. The point is, life is short; we never know what tomorrow holds. I for one, don't want to live my life with any regrets of the things I didn't do, things I didn't accomplish, or chances I didn't take. The world meets no one halfway; it's up to you and only you to get what it is that you want out of life, so go get it!

I used to enjoy helping my grandfather do chores around the farm, and sometimes after our morning chores, we would drive into town to a local tavern and have a sandwich or a pizza for lunch. Shortly before he passed away, when I was fourteen years old, my grandpa bought me my first beer. That's right, I was only fourteen. We lived in Wisconsin, and the drinking age at the time was eighteen, but my grandpa obviously knew the bartender and when he asked if I was old enough, my grandpa replied, "He's my grandson, damn it, if I want to buy him a beer, I can do so." The bartender complied. It was one of the coolest moments of my childhood. My grandpa died a few weeks after that, and I often wonder if he knew his time was coming. He knew life was short, and having a beer with his grandson was obviously something that he wanted to do before he passed.

Never allow yourself to get to a point in your life that you start regretting the things you didn't accomplish, or the risks you didn't take. It's *your* life, and no one else can live it but you. You are in the starring role in your life's story; play that role to the fullest! It's never too soon and it's never too late to go after whatever it is that you want for your life; but it will not happen by accident, and only you can make it happen. Make an action plan and put that plan in motion.

There are lots of great American success stories that didn't begin until later in people's lives. Take the story of Ray Kroc. Ray was in his early fifties, working as a milkshake mixer salesman for Prince Castle Multi-Mixer, whose sales had been plummeting because of lower-priced competition from Hamilton Beach. Kroc took notice of a small local restaurant chain owned by the McDonald brothers, in San Bernardino, California, which had purchased eight of his Multi-Mixer machines for their small restaurant chain. Kroc was impressed with the brothers' unique assembly line method of making good hamburgers. Understanding the franchising potential of McDonald's, Kroc offered to work as a franchising agent for a cut of the profits. Kroc's ambitions, however, ultimately eclipsed those of the McDonald brothers. In 1955, Kroc became president of the McDonald's Corporation, and bought out the owners entirely six years later. In 1977, after leading McDonald's past archrival Burger King, Kroc reassigned himself to the role of senior chairman and held that position until his death in 1984.

In one sense, Kroc's career started at the age of fifteen, when he lied about his age to become a Red Cross ambulance driver in World War I. During his training Kroc met fellow ambulance driver Walt Disney, with whom he would maintain a professional relationship for most of his life. In 1974 at the age of seventy-two, Kroc pursued his lifelong love of baseball and purchased the San Diego Padres baseball team, though he would later proclaim, "There's more future in hamburgers than baseball." Kroc understood that business was only a tool to get what he wanted out of life. His success in business allowed him to pursue his love of baseball.

McDonald's became one of the biggest American business success stories in history, and has maintained its position as the largest restaurant franchise in the world. At the time of Ray Kroc's death, McDonald's had 7,500 locations in thirty-one countries and was worth $8 billion. Kroc died at the age of eighty-one, and at the time his personal fortune was estimated at $500 million.

Another restaurateur who made it big later in life was Harland Sanders, founder of Kentucky Fried Chicken. Sanders is an example of a self-made, rags-to-riches American success story. His father passed away when Sanders was only six years old. Young Harlan soon found himself the man of the family, and by the age of ten began holding down numerous jobs to help support his mom and younger brother and sister.

By the age of forty, Sanders was running a popular service station that also served food to hungry travelers. Sanders had developed a secret recipe, and a method of cooking fried chicken in a pressure pot that allowed it to cook much faster than did the standard methods for frying chicken. Sanders eventually opened a restaurant across the street from the service station, and featured fried chicken so notable that Kentucky governor Ruby Laffoon designated him a Kentucky Colonel, thus naming him Colonel Sanders.

Sanders closed the restaurant in 1952, and at the age of sixty-two years old devoted himself to franchising his fried chicken business. He traveled across the country cooking batches of chicken from restaurant to restaurant, working deals with various restaurant owners who paid him a nickel for every piece of chicken they sold in exchange for using his recipe and cooking method. In 1964, with more than six hundred franchised outlets, Sanders sold his interest in the company for $2 million to a group of Investors. Kentucky Fried Chicken went public in 1966, and was listed on the New York Stock Exchange in 1969. The company was acquired in 1971 by Heublein for $285 million. Heublein subsequently became a subsidiary of RJR Nabisco, and in 1984 PepsiCo acquired Kentucky Fried Chicken for $840 million.

Sanders continued to visit his restaurants around the world as a spokesman in his later years, before he died of leukemia in 1980 at the age of ninety. Sanders always regretted selling his interest in the company.

Colonel Sanders successes helped pave the way for another American success story—that of Dave Thomas, founder of Wendy's. After serving in the U.S. Army during the Korean War, Thomas returned to Fort Wayne, Indiana, and looked up Phil Clauss, his former boss at the Hobby House restaurant. Clauss owned some of the first Kentucky Fried Chicken franchises, and offered Thomas an opportunity to take on some failing restaurants in Columbus, Ohio, and turn them around. A few years later Thomas sold the franchises back to the headquarters for $1.5 million. After complaining that he couldn't find a good hamburger in Columbus, Thomas decided to open his own restaurant in 1969, and named it after his eight-year-old daughter Melinda Lou, known as Wendy. Thomas's marketing genius with his "Where's the beef?" commercials helped make Wendy's among the most successful restaurant chains in the country.

Having been in the restaurant and hospitality business myself for over fifteen years, I have a real appreciation for how tough running a restaurant business is and a real admiration of what Kroc, Sanders, and Thomas accomplished in their lives. In the case of Ray Kroc and Harland Sanders, they were well beyond fifty years of age before they even began to experience entrepreneurial success in life, but they didn't let that slow them down. They both realized that they weren't getting any younger, that life was short, and that if they were going to make it happen they needed to recognize the opportunities before them and take advantage of those opportunities.

My entrepreneurial story began when I was twenty-four years old. I had spent three years as the general manager for a construction company in Kansas City, Missouri, that specialized in insurance restoration. I had just gotten married, and had my first child; my wife was a stay-at-home mom. I had just bought a new house, had two car payments, and was in no position to not have a job. Although I had been making a good living and had a lot of job security, I had a burning desire to make my mark on the world. I was confident that I was making my employer a lot of money and suggested to the owner that he consider making me a business partner; he failed to see the wisdom in that idea, so I offered him my thirty days' notice, and that was that. I left his office, called my wife, and said, "Honey, I just went into business for myself." Needless to say, she wasn't expecting that and had a bit of a panic attack. When my mother found out several weeks later, she was so aggravated at me for not asking for her advice or opinion, and being what she thought was so irresponsible; that she didn't speak to me for nearly a year.

That very same day, I started pounding the pavement trying to stir up some work for my new business, and before the day was out I had secured a contract with the J. C. Nichols management company to repaint multiple apartment units and rebuild some patio decks. This work didn't pay very well, but it did allow me to start hiring a crew of skilled workers while I was pursuing larger, more profitable, construction projects. I would spend the first half of every day working with the crews swinging a hammer and making sure the jobs were going smoothly, then run home, take a shower, and spend the afternoon meeting potential clients and giving estimates.

With nothing more than a pickup truck and a box of tools, I founded Metro Renovators, Inc., in a small office in the back of my garage with a couple thousand dollars that I had managed to save from doing side jobs whenever I could. My new business was a construction company specializing in disaster cleanup and reconstruction. By my second year of business my company had already done more in sales than the company I had left, which had been in business for nearly twenty years. In that first year my company had grown to the point that I had to move out of my home-based operation into a new office facility that I had purchased and renovated in Raytown, Missouri.

Within a couple of years we were rebuilding after natural disasters all over the country. My company had grown to include multiple offices, and before long we had outgrown our Raytown office facility, so I designed and built a new state-of-the-art, 25,000 square foot office and restoration warehouse facility headquartered in Lee's Summit, Missouri.

After going thru a rough divorce, I had pretty much sworn off any chance of ever getting remarried, and vowed to be a confirmed bachelor for the rest of my life. Don't get me wrong, my ex-wife is a good person, and has been a great mom to our kids; it just didn't work for us, and I didn't ever want to risk going thru another divorce again. Never say never. Nine years after I separated from my first wife, I did get remarried. What can I say? Life is short!

This chapter wouldn't be complete if it didn't include the story of how I met my wife. After my divorce, I built a second home at the Lake of the Ozarks, which has ultimately became my hometown. I had planned to spend a three-day weekend at my lake house, and drove down to the lake on a Thursday evening after work. Late that evening, I received a phone call from our Chicago office that we had just received a large reconstruction project that I needed to be at the following day. I decided to get a good night's sleep at my lake house, and head out early the next morning to the Kansas City International Airport to catch an early flight to Chicago. As I was leaving the lake, I stopped at a local gas station. While I was fueling up I talked on my cell phone to my contact person in Chicago, getting an update, when a green pickup truck pulled up on the other side of the fuel pumps. As the door opened and the driver stepped out to fuel up, I literally dropped my cell phone. This was the most beautiful woman I had ever seen! I was immediately smitten as never before. She had her hair in a ponytail pulled through the back of the baseball cap she was wearing, and blue eyes that completely mesmerized me. I tried to smoothly pick up my cell phone, and I swear I never heard another word from the person I was talking to on the other end of the line.

After we had both paid the proprietor of the gas station, whom we both knew by first name, I blurted out, "Stop, wait a minute; I have got to introduce myself to you." We talked for a few minutes, and as it turned out she was working for a local construction company during the day, and also bartended one night a week at a local bar called the Big Easy. She then suggested that I stop by some evening and have a beer. My mind was saying, you bet I'm going to stop by and have a beer! What I failed to hear was that she only tended bar on Saturday nights.

I drove to the airport as quickly as I could, which is worth noting was a good three hour drive from the lake. While I was driving, I contacted my travel agent and made sure I could get a return flight that same day. I had previously intended on staying in Chicago the entire weekend and into the following week to get the project underway, but now I was determined to catch a return flight that Friday evening so I could get back to the lake to stop in and have a beer at the Big Easy. I swear, the moment I left the gas station I called my sister Valerie on the phone and told her that I had just met the woman that I would end up marrying. My sister and I are close, and she was shocked because she'd never heard me say such a thing and knew how I felt about ever remarrying.

I was able to finish up what I needed to do in Chicago and still get back to the lake later that evening. I arrived at the Big Easy at about eleven o'clock. I went in, had a seat at the bar, and ordered a beer, but didn't see the beautiful young lady I had met earlier that day. So I asked the bartender, "Is Dawn working this evening?" Much to my dismay, the bartender replied that Dawn only worked on Saturday evenings. What part of that had I not heard that morning? I had just spent the past sixteen hours running around like a chicken with my head cut off, trying to make sure that I could make it back down to the lake in hopes to further my conversation and possibly ask this woman out, and as it turned out, I could have taken a whole other day to get my work taken care of and still gotten back to the lake at a decent hour on Saturday afternoon.

The rest is history: we went out on our first date the following week, fell head over heels in love with each other, and got married a few years later. Life is short; you have to let it happen, recognize when it does, and accept it with open arms. Some people spend their entire lives searching for love, like it's their mission in life. I had pretty much sworn off love until it hit me upside the head like a ton of bricks in the gravel parking lot of a country gas station.

Eight years after I founded Metro Renovators, I sold the company to Inrecon/Belfor, the world's largest restoration company. I had just turned thirty-two years old. The acquisition made me a multimillionaire overnight, and gave the war chest I needed to pursue other entrepreneurial interests and endeavors. The Inrecon/Belfor acquisition agreement required me to accept a four-year position as the company's regional vice president; which I was glad to accept. I was able to gain a tremendous amount of experience as part of the upper management team of a nationwide organization; it was a very rewarding experience, with some fantastic professional people; whom I could never say enough good things about. When my four-year contract was up I reluctantly declined a lucrative offer to continue my career path with Belfor USA so that I could pursue other business endeavors that I had in the works at the Lake of the Ozarks.

After fulfilling my employment commitment with Belfor USA, I expanded my entrepreneurial aspirations into several different investments and businesses, including; residential & commercial real estate, several restaurants, retail shops, a luxury hotel, a marina; and I have always maintained my primary businesses in construction and development. Six years after leaving Belfor, I had grown my net worth to nearly $40 million dollars.

The economic storm may have started in late 2008, but all of 2009 was a black funnel cloud trying to suck the life out of everything it touched, and destroying everything in its path. Like a tornado coming out of nowhere, the Great Recession hit me like a sledgehammer, and in the blink of an eye I lost the majority of my wealth overnight. I spent the next four years working day in and day out liquidating whatever other assets I could, to eliminate my debt, protect my future; and navigate thru the aftermath of the storm. Miraculously I was able to hold my ground, avoid bankruptcy, and managed to stay alive and keep my good credit intact. I even survived a grueling three year IRS audit. All in all the Great Recession cost me tens of millions of dollars; it was without a doubt a very expensive lesson, but also a very valuable one. I have every intent of taking full advantage of that life lesson in the future.

That what doesn't kill us makes us stronger! Overcoming adversity became my mission in life; I went through the eye of the hurricane and I survived it. I've learned from it, and it has made me a stronger person, a smarter businessman, and a better entrepreneur because of it.

In 2003, I lost one of my very closest friends to a tragic automobile accident; Larry Powell was the Vice President of my design build construction company, and an extremely talented young architect with three beautiful children. Larry and I used to work late into the evenings designing new luxury homes and other construction projects. We had just finished designing the new Tri-County YMCA at the Lake of the Ozarks, and we were both very excited about starting that new project. Larry had everything in his life going in the right direction for him, and everything to live for; then in an instant he was gone. It was one of the hardest and most tragic events of my life, and there still isn't a week that goes by that I don't miss my good friend and wish he was still here. I still keep in touch with his parents and his children when I can, and I know his loss has left a huge hole in their hearts as well. No parent should ever have to bury their children, and no child should ever have to grow up without their father. Life is short, and it can be gone in the blink of an eye, so live your life to the fullest, every day, and don't put things off until tomorrow because tomorrow may never come. As tragic as death is, it is probably what makes life so valuable and so precious. Hug the people you care about often, and never miss an opportunity to tell them how much you care about them.

One valuable lesson I have learned as I approach the age of fifty is that life is short. My two older children, Malari and Merlyn III, are now grown, with aspirations of their own, and there isn't a day that goes by that I don't think about them and miss them. I never was a soccer dad—I was too busy conquering the world of business. It's not that my kids didn't have a great life, and they know without question that I love them very much. But the time I didn't spend with them is time that I can never get back, and there's nothing I wouldn't do to have that time again. My youngest son Gunner is probably the biggest beneficiary of the changes that have occurred in my life and my business since the Great Recession of 2008. He is still at home, so I have a few more good years left with him before he is off to college and then on his own. I know that time will come all too soon. I'm still not a soccer dad, and never will be, but spending quality time with my family has become my number one priority in life.

Had it not been for my getting the wind knocked out of me by the Great Recession, I'm sure that I would still be on the fast track of building and adding to my war chest. Today that's not the most important thing to me. I've made and lost a fortune in my life, but I've managed to hang on to enough to live a very comfortable life. I have no regrets, and can't say in hindsight that I wish I'd done this or that differently.

No doubt there are things that I now recognize that I could have done differently, things that I could have done better. But all of my experiences and all of the challenges that I've faced have led me to where I am today, and I couldn't be happier with where I'm at in my life. I have a great relationship with all of my siblings, I have a beautiful wife whom I love very much, and I have three fantastic children; my two grown children are successful and self-sufficient, and my youngest son is on track to become a productive, self-sufficient young man himself. As for losing most of my wealth; that's part of being in the game. What doesn't kill us makes us stronger, and I'm confident that in the long run I'm much stronger because of the experiences I've been through. I still live as well as I'd ever dreamed I could when I was a young man, and the best is still yet to come!

What is your end game? Where do you want to be in your life five or ten years from now? What's your exit strategy? Are you doing what you want in your life, and with your life? Do you have the education and career you want? Are you preparing for your golden years, and will you have the financial security you need when you are ready to retire? If you own your own business, surely you don't plan on working it every day for the rest of your life. Do you have a succession plan? Have you or are you building a business that would be marketable enough to sell? Do you have children or family members who could take the business over, or have you cultivated key people to take over the business at some point in the future when you are ready to retire? If not, do you have a plan in place to make that happen? Today much of my life is dedicated to helping other business entrepreneurs as a professional business coach and consultant, sharing my life experiences and trying to help other business owners grow their businesses and learn from my successes and challenges. Business has been very good to me, and this is my way of paying it forward. I'm still involved in my construction and development business, and will always be involved in business in some way or another; and I will always be an entrepreneur.

No doubt as my youngest son gets a little older, I will likely jump back into the business arena again on a bigger scale. But for now I have learned to slow down just a little bit and very much appreciate stopping and smelling the roses. Life is short.

I started this book with one simple question, and I hope that these past ten chapters have helped you get closer to answering that question. I hope it's helped you reflect on where your life is at, where it's headed, and what you want out of your life. I hope this book has given you some direction on how to create the life you want for yourself and your family; how to "make it happen". I'll end this book with the same simple question, and remind you that life is short, and the clock is ticking; "**What are you going to do with your one and only life?**"

)Action Steps

1. Your business and career are simply tools to help you get what you want out of life. Identify what's most important to you and what you want out of life.

2. Identify your end game. What do you want later in life?

3. Identify how much income you will need to retire comfortably.

4. What is your plan to reach your goals? Are you on track?

5. Reading this book, may be the last call to action you ever get; take advantage of it today!

Think long and hard about what it is that you truly want out of life. Where do you want to be in the next ten, twenty, thirty, forty, or fifty years and beyond? Are you on track to fulfill your dreams and aspirations? If not, make an action plan today to get you on track!

Write down your responses to these action steps before you close this book. Then review all of your responses to the action steps in each chapter, go back and finish the steps you haven't completed, then prioritize all of them, and immediately start implementing what you think are the top ten action steps that will assist you in your efforts to improve your life and reach your goals. Put all of your Action Steps into action!

Whenever I read any book, or attend any seminar; my one hope and expectation is that I come away with at least one good thought or idea that I can implement to help improve my life or my business. If you got at least one good thought or idea out of this book, I would hope that you found that it was worth the read. If you think your friends, employees, clients, or family would get something positive out of this book; please pay it forward by recommending this book to them, then recommend it via Facebook, LinkedIn, and any other social media.

"What are you going to do now, with the rest of your one and only life?"

Sources & Credits
Chapter One
Alex Manoogian: Masco History
Reese's Peanut Butter Cups: Wikipedia
Madam C.J. Walker (Sarah Breedlove): Bloomberg

Chapter Two
Liebeck v. McDonald's: Time
Sarah McKinley: ABC News
Thomas Montgomery/Internet dating: Stuff.co.nz
Britney Ossenford/Identity theft: CBS News
Roy Pearson v. Soo & Jin Chung/frivolous law suits: Time
Anndorie Sach's/Identity Theft: Orlando Sentinel/WFTV.COM9

Chapter Three
Harley-Davidson: Wikipedia
Steve Jobs/Apple: Biography Tue Story/Wikipedia

Chapter Four
Jack Dorsey/Twitter: Inc.com
Facebook – Mark Zuckerberg/Eduardo Saverin/Cameron & Tyler Winklevoss: Inc.com
Steven Spielberg/Kelsey Grammer/Tiger Woods: Business Leader
Steve Wynn/Kazuo Okada: New York Times

Chapter Five
Richard Branson: Biography True Story/Wikipedia
Sam Walton: Bio True Story

Chapter Six
Walt Disney: Bio True Story
Henry Ford: Mental Flos
Ulysses S. Grant: Mental Flos
Thomas Jefferson: Mental Flos

Abraham Lincoln: Mental Flos
William McKinley: Mental Flos
Roy Raymond/Victoria Secret: Wikipedia/White Orchids

Chapter Eight
911: Wikipedia
Holocaust: Wikipedia
Jim Jones/Jonestown Tragedy: Wikipedia
Monte Teo: ABC News

Chapter Nine
Costa Concordia/Francesco Schettino: Wikipedia/*Guardian*
US Airways Flight 1549/Chesley B. "Sully" Sullenberger: Wikipedia

Chapter Ten
Ray Kroc: Biography True Story
Harland Sanders: Biography True Story
Dave Thomas: Biography True Story

Other Credits: Professional Business Coaches Alliance (PBCA)

A final word from the author & a few photo's

There is no greater satisfaction in life than to be able to do what you love, do it well, and earn a good living at it. I am very proud of a lot of good things that I have "made happen" in my life, for me and my family. I've built several very successful businesses that provided a lot of fulfillment in my life, and financial security for me and my family. I have made a few very good friends along my journey, and most importantly, I have a wonderful family whom I love very much.

I've always had a real love for life, and for really good music; developing a really great restaurant, resort & entertainment complex provided me the opportunity to realize a boyhood dream of being a concert promoter; promoting concerts featuring all of the legendary recording artists that I grew up with and have enjoyed over the years.

Living on the most beautiful lake in the country has made me a real boating enthusiast; which is what motivated me to bring the Offshore Super Series National Championship Powerboat Races to my businesses, and my community. I've always been a motorcycle enthusiast, and there is no better place to ride then the Ozarks; which is why it was important to me to promote another fantastic event for my community, as a founding member of the Lake of the Ozarks Bike Fest.

My passion in life has always been building things; my restoration company has provided me the opportunity to rebuild communities all over America after natural disasters. My design build construction company, has afforded me the ability to design and build some of the most incredible luxury homes in the world. My development company has inspired me to design and build the most beautiful resort developments and community centers in the country.

My love of mother-nature, the great outdoors, and animals has always made me a country boy at heart. You can take the boy out of the country, but you can't take the country out of the boy; since I was nine years old, there has never been a time in my life that I wasn't around horses; it has always been very important to me to instill that same love and appreciation in my children. I always wanted our family homestead to a beautiful log home on a horse ranch out in the middle of the countryside.

The success of my businesses has afforded me the ability to accomplish the things in life that were important to me, and enabled me the ability to provide my family the quality of life that I always wanted them to have. "Business is simply a tool to provide us what we want out of life".

I wanted to share the following photos with you to help bring to life and put into perspective some of the things that have been important to me in my life; things that I have made happen for me and my family. I wish everyone reading this book the greatest success in all of your future endeavors; I wish you and your family; health, wealth, & happiness!

"What are you going to do with your one and only life?"

"The Horny Toad Offshore Super Series National Championship Powerboat Races" –
Merlyn Vandervort, Race Promoter

"The World Famous Horny Toad Entertainment Complex" – Merlyn Vandervort, Founder & Developer

*"The Resort & Yacht Club @ Toad Cove/Camden on the Lake
Resort" – Merlyn Vandervort, Founder & Developer*

"Luxury Homes, Designed & Built by Merlyn Vandervort"

"The Vandervort Family Ranch"

"Merlyn & Dawn Vandervort with Willie Nelson & Steve Miller"

"Merlyn & Dawn Vandervort with the Beach Boys and Charlie Daniels"

"Merlyn & Dawn Vandervort with August Busch and Dale Earnhardt Jr"

"The Vandervort Family"